Jan Chasman

The Keys to Enlightened Living

(Channeled Messages From The Masters)

Channeled by
Rev. Jim Webb

The Keys
to
Enlightened Living

(Channeled Messages From The Masters)

Published by: Prism Publishing, Inc.

ISBN: 0-9663277-3-X

www.revjimwebb.com

This book is dedicated
to the Holy Spirit of GOD,
whose healing power is evident
in this work.

GOD's mercy endureth forever

Acknowledgements

Thanks to Rev. Doris Fochler for her tireless transcriptions of these sessions. Thanks to Rev. Jane Batt and Dr. Dolores Cummings for their constant encouragement and support. Thanks to Rev. Carl Poleskey for his constant support and editing prowess. Thanks also to Ellen Dye and Martha Fischer for their editing. Thanks to Rev. Daniel Neusom for his constant counsel.

Thanks to the participants in these sessions for their courage and faith. Their willingness to grow has created miracles in their lives, and these miracles are now available to others who desire deep transformation.

Thanks to the folks at Signature Books for their patience and support.

Most of all, thank you Mother (*Mrs. Lee Anna Webb 1932-1999*). Love never dies.

www.revjimwebb.com

Table of Contents

Foreword

Since writing "Pathways to Inner Peace" Life-saving Processes for Healing Heart - Mind - Soul, the most frequent questions that people have asked me is "Where did you get the information, processes and tools that have been so useful to me? I was somewhat coy about the source of the information, because I didn't believe that the mass audience would be comfortable with the source. Therefore, I was reluctant to tell people that the source for much of the information was channeled by a group of beings who work through me (The MASTERS of Planetary Healing and Transformation).

However, the next-most frequently asked question was "how do I employ these Pathways successfully in my everyday life? To answer this question, I didn't have to look any further than the lives of the people who were present during these channeled sessions. The participants were able to transform their lives in astounding ways by working with the information. However, providing insights into how the participants used the information required me revealing more about the source of the information. Finally, I had to come out as a channel. However, due to the success of the Conversations With GOD series of books, a mass audience is more comfortable with channeled information, and there are many more light workers who also want to move deeper onto their spiritual path.

As a result, I am submitting "The Keys to Enlightened Living" to you so that you, too may realize the benefits, blessings and gifts of Grace that are inherent in the words and energies within this book. I hope it helps you in the way that this information has already helped others. Be blessed and in GOD.

Rev. Jim Webb (www.revjimwebb.com)

CHAPTER 1.

MEET THE MASTERS

THE MASTERS OF PLANETARY HEALING AND TRANSFORMATION (THE MASTERS) are a collective of "energy" that emanates from the heart of GOD. This "energy" provides guidance, insights, tools and healing energy to transform individuals' consciousness (and thus to transform the planet's collective consciousness). This "energy" accesses my consciousness, my experiences and my motor skills to communicate divine wisdom that will facilitate the healing and transformation of humans and humanity. Repeatedly, THE MASTERS have been asked "who are you?" and the answer is consistent – a collective of energy that vibrates at different frequencies and velocities based on the needs of the recipient. They frequently give the example that "you wouldn't call a foot doctor for a heart problem, and you wouldn't call a heart doctor for a foot problem". Therefore the "energy" vibrates with a frequency that is appropriate for the task at hand. The "energy" is infinite, and thus is reluctant to take a finite form (such as a name). However, at certain times (when pressed) the "energy" has taken a finite form or a name, because the recipient believed strongly that the "energy" HAD to take a finite form to be understood, embraced and contacted. When this has occurred, the "energy" chose the most pertinent name, and reminded all that this name represented a specific portion of the continuum of energy that was coming through my channel.

How Does This Process Work?

I have one of the easiest jobs in the world – I fall asleep. During my nap, I feel a great bliss, a sublime peace, and a wonderful healing energy. When I awaken, I am refreshed and energized. During this process, the MASTERS access my consciousness, my motor skills, my experiences and my voice to communicate the wisdom and guidance that can help you to grow spiritually, experience more peace and bliss, and to live always in the presence of GOD's unconditional love.

This process (called channeling) is the same process that Edgar Cayce used to bring divine wisdom to the earth. As humanity has evolved, and as the "New Age" has come upon us, we understand more about channeling than we ever have. Channeling is simply bringing information "through" a human being from a divine source.

To understand the process of channeling, it is important to understand that we all have access to another realm of information and energy. We cannot see this realm of information and energy with our human eyes. We cannot hear it with our human ears. We cannot feel it with our outer senses. However, we all know that this unseen realm exists (just as we know that magnetism and gravity exist even though we only see their effects). When we attune our "inner senses" through prayer and meditation, we can access this information. In prayer (speaking to GOD) and meditation (listening to GOD), we deprive our outer senses. As a result, our inner senses become more developed in the same way that a blind person has a more acute sense of hearing (one sense has become more developed to compensate for the loss of another sense). By exercising prayer and meditation, we develop our "inner senses" in the same way that we develop our heart muscles and our biceps through physical exercise. As our "inner senses" become more attuned, the information superhighway that we build between our physical world and the spiritual world can carry more information.

Initially, we may get brief "flashes of insights" or "hunches". The initial "hunches" may not be different from the "coincidences" that we have all experienced, such as when we have a strong thought about someone and get a phone call from them within minutes. However, as our experience (and our ability to trust) grows, we get more and more information. In other words, the information superhighway between our human consciousness and the divine consciousness can carry more traffic. We may experience more explicit information such as seeing scenes happening in our mind's eye, hearing words or phrases with our inner ear, or having deep feelings of instant "knowing".

As this process continues, we learn to suspend our human perception and "receive" information with our "spiritual antenna". As our "spiritual antenna" gets more practice, we can pick up stronger and stronger signals. We then learn to suspend our human consciousness and let the divine consciousness come through in a clearer way, without the distortions caused by our human fears and doubts. Finally, we may learn to fall asleep and bring though this consciousness. When "asleep" we most certainly have suspended our human consciousness even more, so that divine beings can access our consciousness to bring more divine wisdom to the earth.

This path of opening to channel is available to all of us, and is no great mystery. In my particular case, this path has also included the emotional healing necessary to ensure that my own "stuff" wasn't coming through and contaminating the divine wisdom. The process of emotional healing that I outline in my first book, ***"Pathways to Inner Peace: Lifesaving Processes for Healing Heart, Mind and Soul"*** is an important part of the process, because as we raise our vibration (by releasing our emotional baggage) our information superhighway can accommodate more information from a higher level of consciousness.

Therefore, I always pray that the information that comes through my channel is clear and undistorted and that the information comes from the highest source available. I hope that as you read this book, the information transforms you in the same way that it has transformed others who participated.

CHAPTER 2

AN OVERVIEW

"And The Last Shall Be The First"

The information that you are about to receive is the result of approximately 6 months of channeled sessions I gave weekly. The recipients of these sessions received (and worked with) the tools to facilitate their rapid spiritual growth and transformation with wonderful results. In the words of one recipient "I have been transformed physically, emotionally and psychically as a result of these sessions. My life has opened in a wonderful way financially, and I have found a peace that I didn't even know existed."

At certain points in the process, it became clear that the group had reached a new level. As a result, THE MASTERS would pause and review what had been learned and accomplished. One of these summaries provides an excellent overview of what will be covered in subsequent chapters of this book. Therefore, I have provided this sample transcript (with slight editing to make it easier to read) as an overview to "The Keys To Enlightened Living". The Chapters that follow are also transcripts from these sessions (with slight editing to make the book more readable).

MASTERS: Do you feel the joy and peace in this room tonight?

Group: Yes.

MASTERS: Do you feel the love in this room tonight?

Group: Yes.

MASTERS: This is YOU! This is your essence. This is your birthright. This is your natural state. This is the norm. The way that you usually feel will become the exception as you move deeper and deeper into the light. The bliss you feel right now is simply and only a hint of those things to come as you move into alignment with the energy of unconditional love that is GOD. As you progress, you will sustain these feelings of bliss for extended periods of time, even while you are immersed in your physical world because you have done something quite courageous. You have submitted your consciousness and your ego to the consciousness of GOD for healing and transformation, so that you may return to the Heart of GOD. You will return to the state of being that is of GOD – the wonderful state of bliss, peace and love. We congratulate you on your journey. We congratulate you on all of the work that you have done on yourselves in opening to our light and letting our light do its job, which is to transform you. By doing your part in this process, you have opened in a wonderful way. And so tonight, it is our honor and our pleasure to welcome you to a new level of existence.

We talked about initiation before. We began sharing with you the truth that initiations happen at any time in small increments. Tonight is one of those initiations. All of you now understand your mastery, your unlimited nature and your ability to bear light at a deeper level. You know that your task is to use this light for your greatest good and for the greatest good of the earth. Tonight we offer you encouragement to continue moving deeper and deeper into the light through your own connections to our light, which have been firmly established. You can maintain this connection through your own individual prayers and meditations, and in the group prayers and meditations that are given in places such as this. As you continue with your prayers and meditations you will continue to expand.

We would continue our talk with you tonight by recapping some of the key points that we have covered. We covered opening to light (which is spiritual growth), realizing and nurturing the light that lives within you, and letting it grow to the point where it subsumes the false-ego (which is the portion of your consciousness that does not yet recognize its divinity). As we have said, the false-ego is attached to the trappings of the earth that would give it validation based on outward things (such as wealth, physical shape, physical abilities, athletic prowess, intelligence and socio-economic status). These trappings of the false-ego ignore the beauty, power and unlimited ability that lies within each individual by looking only at the outward manifestation of the individual. You have seen how destructive that the false-ego can be. You have learned that surrendering to the lure of the false-ego is tantamount to denying the true self – which is the self which lives within – which is the self that is perfect, beautiful, lovable, and whole. You have learned this lesson well.

You have also learned of your path of spiritual expansion into the light, and that your energy attracts its reflection and reflections of different aspects of your consciousness at all times. You have learned that if there is a part of your consciousness that you are not yet ready to accept, when you see it reflected in another, you reject the other person. Your **TRUE** task is then to learn that your lesson is to accept every part of your consciousness. Your true task is to evolve every part of your consciousness so that it moves out of the illusion that sees only the false-ego, so that it moves into the truth of your innocence and your perfection. When this occurs, you see only the innocence and perfection of others as well, and you move more FULLY into a place of self acceptance. So you have learned that in relating, your task is to see where your reflections of yourself are aligned with the simple truths of GOD's unconditional love for you, the universe's unconditional support for you, and your ability to love and accept yourself completely and unconditionally. **Therefore, relationships are designed to teach you where you are loving yourself and where you are not.**

Therefore, **each relationship is holy** – from the briefest one to the most long-lasting one, for they are all designed to reflect aspects of your consciousness that must be healed by being aligned with unconditional love. For as you vibrate more and more with unconditional love, you are able to absorb more of our light, for it becomes more compatible with you. This is how you grow spiritually.

You have also learned about relationships that are of a sexual nature. They, too are deeper ways for you to move into unconditional loving acceptance for yourself. They are deeper ways for you to move out of the world of your illusion and into the world of our reality. For sexual expression in any way - and in any form - is simply the body's way of expressing, feeling, and experiencing joy, bliss and the elation of ecstasy. And what is GOD but the expression of joy, bliss and the elation of ecstasy? When you judge yourself negatively or when you judge others negatively regarding sexuality or any dimension, you are denying a part of the self, and you are not in full, unconditional loving acceptance for yourself. So you learn that sexual expression in any way - in any form – is not unlike singing, breathing, learning, laughing, or otherwise experiencing joy. Sexual expression (in your world of illusion) has many things attached to it: judgment, shame, fear, and guilt. Those are illusions. As you explore, expand and experience the bliss that you are to manifest through sexual expression, you expand your ability to attract more and more bliss to you. You become more comfortable living in a state of bliss, and that how the soul expands.

We also explored the reasons why those attachments or taboos have been associated with sexuality and sexual expression. The dominant consciousness on the earth (for many lifetimes) has sought to keep individuals from experiencing and expressing their GOD-selves in order to control individuals. The suppression and the stigmatization of sexual expression was a part of the process of control. So as you move forward and you explore your relationships with others, you explore them on many levels. One level on which you explore your ability to love yourself completely and unconditionally is through sexual expression. It is one of an infinite number of avenues and ways that you may express and experience the joy that is your divine birthright and your natural state. So in your practices, your task (if you choose) is to see how much, how long and how deeply you may experience the bliss of your sexuality. For as you expand your capacity to experience this bliss, of course, you expand your capacity to experience ALL realms of bliss and you expand your ability to experience the Kingdom of Heaven here on earth, which is a realm of bliss.

If you recall the energies that you experienced at the beginning of this session, were they not unlike the energies of sexual bliss? They were very similar to sexual bliss. Therefore, the lesson that we would teach you in summary, is that GOD's light is not separated from any aspect of your life. GOD's light is fully present as you allow it into any aspect of your life. It can heal, transform and expand any and every aspect of your life as you use it to do so.

You have also learned a lesson in self-responsibility as you have walked your path. You have learned that your task while you are here on earth is to simply expand your consciousness, experience the bliss of this expansion, create with the power that this expansion provides and experience that which you create. In doing this, you expand the light of GOD. You have learned that you – and you alone -- are responsible for this. Each individual is responsible for this individually, for as you serve yourself in this way, you serve others as well, for what greater service can you give to others than to increase their capacity to unleash the GOD-light that lives within them too?

However, each individual must be responsible for themselves. For if the individual is not responsible for himself or herself, then that individual is not actualized, and is not creating or taking responsibility for their own creations. Therefore, the individual is not expanding in divine intent. By taking responsibility for someone else you are not only denying that person their own divinity, but you are denying your own, for you are not focusing on your own growth. The notion of self-responsibility is a difficult notion to grasp, because it is inconsistent with the dominant consciousness that has created the world of illusion in which you live. As you work with this in your super-human mind through your prayers and meditations, the truth of it will become quite apparent to you.

So in coming full-circle, you have learned through these sessions how to grow your light. You have learned through these sessions what illusions keep you from expanding your light and you have learned how to counteract any illusions that stand between you and GOD. The door is now open for you. The light from the heart of GOD touches you now, and as you choose, you may move more deeply into the light of GOD – into the heart of GOD. Be blessed and be in GOD as you move forward.

❧❧❧❧

Author's Comments

WOW. Some pretty interesting and somewhat controversial notions. These, and other concepts will be explained more fully as you read further. However, after a discourse like this one, THE MASTERS open the session for questions from the group. In the session that you have just read, the questions that were asked help to give you a further introduction to the Channeled Messages because they offer an overview of additional Keys To Enlightened Living that will be covered more fully in this book.

❧❧❧❧

Question: Thank you so much for the many, many wonderful lessons given to us during these sessions. Many of us in this forum are still dealing with prosperity issues as we practice the truths channeled from you. Would you please comment on that?

MASTERS: Yes we would. We would first discuss the nature of prosperity, and we would then discuss how to enhance your ability to prosper. We would then share with you additional techniques for unblocking yourselves from the blessings that are always being showered upon you.

An Overview

Prosperity, as you know, begins with your energy and your vibration. As you raise your energy and as you raise your vibration, you become magnetized to draw to you more freely (and without blockages) that which you desire. Your process of working on yourselves (which each of you does quite well) helps you to naturally enhance your ability to attract your desires and therefore to become more prosperous.

The process of emotional release is important as well. When you create things in your life by sending out a request to the universe, you may inadvertently attach the energy of fear to that request. You may subconsciously believe that the request would not be granted or that you would suffer terribly due to an undercurrent of guilt that you have about the request. When this occurs, there is an invisible energy of fear that is attached to the request that makes it more difficult to manifest the desire. The energy that is sent out (which is like a clenched fist) is not compatible with the energy of GOD (which is like an open palm, waiting to give to you). Emotional release disbands the energies of fear, anxiety and worry so that they are no longer attached to the request. When these energies are no longer attached to the request it is easier for the request to manifest on the earth plane.

So we would say to you, individually you are doing quite well in your process of release. Therefore, you will do quite well in your process of drawing to you that which you desire. Know that individually you may move through what you might consider to be a period of darkness so that these fears, anxieties and angers can dissipate. Then your energy will glow in a very magnificent way with its true power, and you will bring to you all that you desire. You may choose to write your desires on paper. You may then begin to release any subconscious feelings that may be attached to the desires by asking "are there any hidden fears attached to these desires?" and you will be shown where you are creating out of either fear or self-rejection. You can then release the fear emotionally and burn the paper. As you burn the paper, you symbolically send out the energy of release. When the fears and doubts are released, try not to take them back. Do not release as if you are casting a fishing pole on the water, for when you cast a fishing pole, there is a string attached.

Release as if you are releasing a beautiful dove – and giving that dove its freedom. For when you give a dove its freedom, then and only then can the dove manifest its full beauty and grace.

Comment: Thank you.

MASTERS: Yes. Be blessed. And please, for a moment, take in this energy that comes from our Creator.

Author's Comments

THE MASTERS frequently pause to send healing energy to be absorbed by the participants. As you read this, you may choose to meditate briefly so that you may absorb that same healing energy.

Question: You have mentioned this before, but maybe a brief recap can help me. How can you get rid of your fears?

MASTERS: The process of releasing your fears begins with your mind. You must first know that there is a power, energy and great love. You perceive this power, energy and love to be outside of you. This force sustains you, protects you, supports you, nourishes you and nurtures you. You may continue to perceive this energy through your prayers and meditations, for prayer and meditation will open the channel between you and this energy that you perceive outside of you. As you work with this process, you feel more physical manifestations of this energy. You see this energy manifesting in every aspect of your life. This energy can permeate deep levels of your consciousness. Little by little this energy BECOMES your consciousness. This is the energy of GOD, and it moves out any fears.

You can help this process by saying "I am afraid" - and listing those things that you are afraid of. When you feel the fear, you may scream, moan, or express your fears in any way that won't harm you or anyone else. Because your are releasing your fear during prayer and meditation, you have invited the energy of GOD into your energy field so that it can take these fears and transform them. The energy of GOD moves the fears out of your energy field and replaces them with a feeling of peace and security. Do not deny these fears for that will not release you from them. Acknowledge your fears. You do not have to be ashamed to acknowledge your fears for they are an illusion, and as you work to release your fears they are taken from you.

We would offer you this prayer to repeat right now.

Mother Father GOD, please release me from my fears for my fears do not give my peace. Your will for me is to have peace. My will for me is to have peace. I align my will with thy will, and I give you permission to remove from my energy anything that would cause me fear. I ask you to heal my mind, body and affairs so that I know only your peace. I cast my fears upon the waters, for my fears are like crumbs of bread, and they are lost in the infinite ocean of your love. They are taken away by the infinite currents of your love. They are dissolved by the infinite power of your love. So I release to you my fears. AMEN.

Comment: Thank you.

MASTERS: You are very welcome. Know that we are with you here and always. Know that we support you. Know that we affirm you when others seem not to. Know of your goodness. Know of your graciousness. Know of your strength. Know of your brilliance. Know of your ability. You do not have to apologize to anyone. You do not have to feel "less than". You do not have to fear, for the light of GOD within you is brilliant and powerful and complete and resourceful and creative and strong and masterful.

Know that these descriptors also describe you.

CHAPTER 3.

THE NATURE OF GOD

MASTERS: It is with pleasure, and honor, and joy that we serve you in this way this evening. We would first like to congratulate those of you who choose to continue with this process. We would observe your courage. We would observe and applaud your strength and vision. We would congratulate you on the growth that you have exhibited as you have opened to the Light of GOD that has always been available to you. And we will discuss the light of GOD in more detail.

For those of you who are beginning this process in this way tonight, we welcome you with open arms to a place that does not judge you, that does not measure you, that does not pit you one against the other, but simply moves to acknowledge the Light of GOD that lives within you.

We would then proceed with what is GOD? And we would offer you a paradox:

GOD is everything, yet GOD is nothing.

We would elaborate on this by saying to you that in your human mind, and with the human consciousness, which is but a limited portion of the infinite consciousness that is the "all," there has been an attempt to define the energy of GOD in finite terms that are understandable with the limited human consciousness.

These attempts are futile, however, in that there are no limited terms to describe something that is unlimited. So we say again, "GOD is everything, and GOD is nothing." For GOD is simply the "all," all matter, all anti-matter, all consciousness, all reflections of consciousness. What you see as people, places or things, the planets, the heavens, and "all," -- it is all consciousness. And this collective is GOD. This collective is **one**. It is all unified. However, GOD, for this collective, expresses in many different ways. For you see, the tree outside of this building is an expression of part of the consciousness of the whole. This building is itself an expression of this consciousness of the whole. **You** are individualized expressions of this consciousness of the whole.

You may choose to separate and categorize yourself from those things which seem to be less alive, such as a tree, or those things that seem to be not alive at all, such as a building. But the common matter that you all share is the matter of neutrons, protons, electrons. And what makes the neutrons, protons and electrons do what they do? What makes them spin? What makes them vibrate? What keeps them together? What gives them different densities? What gives them different qualities? What gives them different ways of reflecting light? We will tell you! The light that is **within** them reflects the light and bends the rays of light in different ways. So they appear to be different. But the common denominator is that they are made of Light - spiritual energy - particles of the whole that have yet to be truly defined, but exist nonetheless. Your science is getting closer and closer to defining this energy.

As some of you know, there have been studies that indicate that the body loses ounces of weight at the time of death. And that the ounces of weight that the body loses is the soul, or spiritual energy, that has infused the body with the life force. There have been other indications that this unseen substance exists. As, at one point your scientists believed that neutrons, protons and electrons were the smallest parts of matter.

Now that is no longer the case. You experience this unseen matter, this unseen energy, this unseen force. You experience it in your prayers and in your meditations. You sometimes have trouble defining exactly what it is, but you know that it **is.** Well, that which "**is,**" is a part of everything. And everything is a part of that which "**is**". But everything expresses in a different way.

We will use an analogy that we have used before -- the analogy of water. Water in its liquid form is water. However, as the vibratory rate of the water slows down, the water becomes ice, and it seems to have different qualities. It seems to be solid instead of liquid, like your chair appears to be solid instead of liquid. But you know that its essence is unchanged. On the other hand, as the vibratory rate of the water increases, the water becomes vapor, and it has different qualities as well. It no longer seems to be liquid, nor solid. It appears to be gaseous, and it has different qualities. It appears to be lighter than air, and it appears to float. Yet you know that its essence is essentially unchanged. By the same token, you, the tree, and the building appear to have different qualities, yet you have the same essence. You, and your sister, or your brother next to you appear to have different qualities, yet you have the same essence. So again we say to you, GOD is everything, and GOD is nothing.

So we would move forward in our explanation. For the thing that makes you all essentially the same is the light of GOD, which holds your seemingly individual neutrons, protons and electrons together, that infuses you and infuses everything. GOD is everything, yet GOD is nothing. This force has created many, many expressions. They are **all** of the force. This force is pure, unconditional love. So that which this force has created in its reflection are also seemingly individual manifestations of unconditional love.

So **you** are a manifestation of unconditional love. GOD is everything, yet GOD is nothing. You cannot point to a single thing and say "that is GOD, or this is GOD." But you look around and you know that everything is GOD. ***GOD is simply the energy and consciousness of unconditional love.***

So you may ask "If this is truth, why do I not think and behave in this way?" And we will answer you. You have believed that you are separate from each other, AND from other expressions of GOD's unconditional love. You have been taught that you were separate from GOD. That GOD was this being, this caricature, which was vengeful, judgmental, punishing, and controlling. And you believed it. You forgot that GOD is everything, and **you** are a part of that everything, and that you have all the qualities of GOD. Yet you have retained some of these qualities. You retained the quality to create in the same way that the collective consciousness has the ability to create. So you have created experiences, and an existence, that is based on what you believe. You have created this existence where you believe in separateness so you experience separateness. Where you believe in a judgmental and punitive GOD. You experience what you believe is GOD's judgment and punishment because you believe that there is an outer force that dictates your experiences. You have forgotten that in truth the only thing that dictates your experiences is the inner force within you that **is** GOD.

Now we come to bring you good news. This news is not new for some of you, yet it is always ever so important to reinforce in every way. The good news is that **you are GOD**. Those who have told you that GOD is outside of you have done so because of their lack of understanding. Because they were told that untruth and they believed it. And they have created with that. But you are now knowing the new truth. You know this. You feel this. You are experiencing it. And with this new truth, you know that you have all the qualities of GOD, all the rights of GOD, and all the responsibilities of GOD. The qualities of GOD are:

- An ability to love completely and unconditionally;
- Perfection;
- Fullness;
- Infinite Intelligence;
- Infinite Power.

As you embrace this, as you meditate on it, as you **live** it, as you let this truth seep into every cell of your being, and every portion of your energy field, your intelligence grows, your energy field grows, because more of the collective can be contained within your energy field. You become more in union with GOD, realigned with the energy of the collective. This is growth and development. This is your birthright. This is the truth that you are opening to now. So we will pause for a moment and we will let our words seep into your energy field. So please prepare to receive our Light.

Now this truth has seeped into a deeper level of your consciousness, and we now will continue.

These teachings may seem radical to some of you. To others, these teachings confirm what you already know in a slightly different way. You do not have to force yourself in any way to adopt something, a line of thinking, a line of being, that you are not ready to adopt. For you have free will, and you have all the time in eternity.

What you must ask yourself is, "If I can accept that I create my experiences, based on the energy that I contain and what I believe, and if I can change those beliefs to create a new experience for myself, am I not mastering my earthly environment? Am I not doing something that seems to be out of the realm of human capabilities? Am I not working with a higher power?"

The answer is, of course, yes. You are. That higher power that you are accessing is the higher power that has lived with you in all ways at all times. You are just acknowledging that which exists. And through acknowledging it, you are bringing it more to the surface, and using it in a more conscious way for your betterment and for the betterment of the earth.

By choosing this consciousness, you are drawing to you, more of that energy that you perceive outside of yourself. You are simply opening to the truth of that which is outside of you is your creation, and is of GOD, and that which is inside of you is your creation, which is GOD. You are blurring the distinction between them. For you know that it is all a part of GOD's consciousness. It is all one. And it is all available to you.

Now we will take this one step further. And we would say if all is GOD, and all is a part of you, for you are a part of GOD, and GOD is a part of you, then that which is GOD's belongs to you and belongs to everyone. For all is part of the collective. And this is not the communist manifesto, this is a truth. And so, you then can open yourself to the riches of the universe. For what is GOD's belongs to you, and is your due, and what is GOD's belongs to everyone, and is his or her due.

When you open yourself to this truth, you understand the infinity of the universe. And that there are an infinite number of possibilities or probabilities awaiting you. Therefore, you needn't have a fear of lack. You also needn't have fear because you know that there is no force outside of you that would punish you or cause you pain and suffering. You know also that all the collective wants to do is to create and to expand, and to expand and to create.

The collective wants to see how many colors, how many experiences, how many words, how many deeds, how many acts of laughter, how many expressions of joy, how many manifestations of peace can be created. For each manifestation magnifies the whole. You then understand that your task is simply to understand who you are. Your task is to understand that you are a seemingly individualized expression of the whole. The whole continually expands.

As you open to more and more of your understanding of your part of being in the whole, and as you understand that you have all the qualities of the whole as a seeming subset of the whole, then you live with peace, and joy, and comfort, and bliss, and union and enlightenment. This consciousness differs from your current understanding, which believes in pain, suffering, lack, and denigration and struggle. The choice is always yours.

We offer, if you choose, a different way to view the world, and a different way to view yourself, and a different way to view GOD that is more affirming to you, and is more in line with the truth of GOD. This is a very complex topic. For as we said before, GOD is everything, and GOD is nothing. In truth, GOD is the energy of unconditional Love.

This is a very abstract concept for the rational human mind to grasp, which is why humans have struggled to personify GOD. So how do you define everything, and how do you define nothing? How do you place that which is so infinite in terms that are so finite? You don't. You attempt to, and then you send energy so that the truth may be absorbed on a cellular level. So we will work with your energy now so that you may digest that which we have given you in a way that is palatable for you, and for your greatest good. So please prepare to receive our energy. And we thank you. And we will open this session to your questions.

Question: I'll ask one. You were talking earlier about GOD as the infinite and the provider of all. And I for one would like to get off the train of lack. Is this my creating the situation, or am I along on the ride of someone else's creation?

MASTERS: We would draw your attention, first of all, back to one of the key understandings that is necessary for you to understand truly who you are as an individual expression of GOD's consciousness. That key understanding is that you, and you alone, are creating your situation. And you, and you alone, must be responsible for it and take responsibility for it. We would share with you some words of assurance here, because that is sometimes a very difficult lesson to master, and that is sometimes a very difficult lesson to accept. For in the way the human consciousness works, responsibility often equates to blame. For when situations are not working out in a way that would appear to be acceptable, blame is assigned.

We would clarify by sharing with you that responsibility is not blame. For blame is a word of judgment. Blame implies that there is something wrong with the situation. And from a human perspective, there may appear to be something wrong, for you experience lack. But from the perspective of GOD's consciousness, the experience is a catalyst for opening to a new truth, which heals your consciousness. For in experiencing lack, you realize that there is a part of your consciousness that is not aligned with the infinity of GOD's consciousness, which is infinite. As you open in prayer, in emotional release, and in every way possible to a shift in your perception, you align more and more with the consciousness of GOD, which is the consciousness of abundance.

From that perspective, this is not something to blame. For this is a wonderful gift. It is a gift of having a guidepost (the experience of lack) that would help point you in the direction of GOD's unconditional love. Therefore, there is no need to judge the situation. Ultimately, there is a need to give thanks for this situation. For this situation has helped to put you on what we will not call the "right track", for that would be judgment, but it has helped to move you along in your path of aligning every thought, and therefore everything you create, with the truth of GOD. And so we would say to you, do not assign blame in any way when you think of taking responsibility. For taking responsibility is not taking "the blame." For there is nothing to blame.

Taking responsibility is making the statement "Yes, I have created this situation. And, wow, look how powerful I am! Look at what a powerful situation I have created! But, look at how I can create an even more powerful situation for me that is affirming, that is aligned with GOD's energy, that is the energy of creation. And I can create an even more wonderful situation for myself. So I take responsibility for what I have created in the past." You may say "Yes, I take responsibility for what I have created in the past, but yes, I also take responsibility, and therefore I take power. And with that power, I create what I desire here and now, and as I move forward, in what you would call time. So that is a different way of looking at the situation.

As you continually, continually look **past** what you perceive as limiting factors, and look **to** GOD as the source, and as you understand that the source is infinite, then you will not **only** look in the places where you are looking now for your abundance. For more and more conduits for your abundance will open. And if those conduits are not where you believe they are now, they are elsewhere in the infinity of GOD. For you are responsible, yet you have the power. So do not believe for a moment that there is a force outside of you which has created your situation.

If you are deeply intertwined with a consciousness that is not vibrating in a way that would enable more and more Light to come in and, then you must change your consciousness and open to the infinite energy of GOD to provide an unlimited number of ways for your abundance to manifest. **There are as many ways for your abundance to flow to you as there are stars in the sky, or grains of sand on the beach, or waves in the ocean.** So look not to those finite sources that you believe are the sources of your supply and your infinite abundance. Look only to GOD. And leave much of this task to GOD. Let the Infinite Intelligence, Wisdom and Power of GOD bring to you that which you desire through whichever delivery mechanisms are in your greatest good.

Also, look at **how** you are creating. What you may be doing is sending out an energy that has an erroneous belief attached to it. The energy that you may be sending out in certain instances is an energy that says, "GOD, I am open and I am desirous of more abundance." However attached to that energy may be an energy of fear. The subtext is "I am open to and desirous of more abundance, because I am afraid and I truly do not believe that you will provide for me." And that may not be the most productive way to send out the request because it sends out an erroneous belief. Therefore, that error is reflected to you. So instead, release the fear to GOD's Light in every way possible for you.

For your specific purposes, release the fear, surrender the fear to GOD, get in touch with the emotional body, and get in touch with the fear, and let it cycle through you. Then, instead of sending out the request in what might be considered a male-aggressive way, open yourself for the shower of Light in a female-passive way. This change in your energy pattern changes the dynamic. And understand that we will continually work with you. Understand that you will be provided for. Understand that you are loved. Understand that you are not being judged. Understand that you are being guided in a very meticulous way to the truths that would bring you peace, and you are in the process of discarding untruths that do not bring you peace. And this process is a beautiful process ultimately, for it is not unlike the unfolding of a flower. Have faith and trust that this process is guided by Divine Love. And blessed be you.

Question: I seem to have trouble meditating. I don't know if it is the discipline of it, or the isolation of it. There is something I need to work through with meditation. I need some help with that.

MASTERS: We would say to you that the reinforcement of a group would be useful for you. For it would help you to begin to focus on this task in a deeper way. We would also suggest to you that you work physically on this process through walking, and choosing a wooded path that is free of urban distractions. For you see, the environments that you are using to attempt meditation are environments that are full of your issues. You are constantly being bombarded by your issues in your attempts. By **removing** yourself from that environment, you automatically remove yourself from a great deal of the energy that would keep you from focusing. As you **physically** place yourself in a different realm, it becomes easier for you to **mentally** place yourself in a different realm. We would also add that this action has other positive physiological benefits.

We would then suggest that you focus on a thought. You may call it a mantra. You may call it a core affirmation that you choose, such as "I love myself completely and unconditionally." And you may begin by using your (walkman). As you work with repeating these words like a mantra, you can continually focus your thoughts on these words every time your mind drifts. This is physical action, this physical removal from your environment, and this continual reinforcement of a central thought or theme will help to condition your mind to focus. This may help you. You are blessed. You will find that as you work with this method of developing discipline, it will be easy for you, and you will take off like a bird in flight.

Question: Why is it so difficult to stay with the process of self love and self acceptance, and to eliminate self criticism and self judgment. It seems to be difficult for me not to revert back to those things. Is there some fear that keeps them in place that I am not aware of?

MASTERS: Why is it difficult to walk in the rain and not get wet? You see, you are constantly being bombarded by signals and information that is not loving, that is not affirming, that is not in truth. We will give you a simple example.

A commercial in the Channel's consciousness is, "ring around the collar." In the unenlightened decade of the 60's, the commercial took the form of a housewife, a domestic GODdess, whose husband had ring around the collar. When the husband found out that he had ring around the dollar, the husband gave the wife a dirty look. The wife shrank in shame. The message was that you should feel shame and inadequacy if you do not fit this erroneous standard of perfection and always get rid of ring around the collar. Many products are sold through subtle shaming mechanisms that continually bombard you consciousness with the untruth that you are unworthy, and that you are unlovable, and that you are not enough, and that you are not whole, and that you are not full (unless you buy the product). In other words, shame was used to sell a form of salvation.

So we ask again, why is it difficult to walk in the rain without getting wet? For you are constantly being bombarded by images that would promote your self-hatred and self-rejection, and would not enable you to develop more self love. Your umbrella, your raincoat, your galoshes, your ski suit that keeps you dry and warm is the truth of GOD. Your task is to monitor every possible thought and to examine and become conscious of every thought that you have. And you may find that some of them do not reflect the simple truths that we have shared with you before, and that we will share with you again.

The simple truths are:

- **GOD loves you completely and unconditionally;**
- **The universe supports you completely and unconditionally;**
- **You have permission to love yourself completely and unconditionally.**

So think of every thought that you have as a raindrop. Every time you feel a raindrop, ask yourself, "Where is my thinking not aligned with the simple truth?" You will find the answer. At that moment, pray that your mind be healed. Pray that your consciousness be shifted. Pray that you be transformed at that moment from that unaffirming thought, or that unaffirming belief, and that your thought be aligned with the simple truth. In this process of continual prayer, which we would call ***constant communion***, you continually build an energy and a flow between your energy field and the Heart of GOD, or the Core of Creation, from which all has emanated.

This flow that you continually build strengthens you. It makes your umbrella bigger. It makes your raincoat stronger. It makes your galoshes more impenetrable. For each time you do it, you draw to you more of the truth, and you move out of you more of that which is not in truth.

Little by little, you start vibrating with that which is the truth. As you vibrate more and more with the truth, as you bring in more Light, you draw to you situations that are reflective of your new Light. The process gets easier, and easier, and easier, and you become impervious to the raindrops of consciousness that are around you. For they have no power over you. For they are no longer your truth, and you no longer buy into them. This is the process. It is an ongoing process. It is a constant process. As you open to GOD more and more, you simply give GOD permission to heal your mind. And every time you have an unaffirming thought, you give GOD permission to heal your mind. You say, "It is my will for myself to be healed, for I desire peace." And the process continues. Prayer and meditation, where you are continually bathed in the Light helps the process considerably. For when you know that the light comes to you in such great volume, and moves through you in such great volume, and when you experience that joy and that bliss, you truly understand that this is the Bliss of GOD. If you were not of GOD, then this energy would not be working through you. If you were unworthy and unlovable, then the unconditional love that flows through you would be unable to flow through you. So you then deeply and truly understand in a deeper way that you are loved completely and unconditionally. For you feel it. And you experience it. Then you see the world as an illusion, and you release the pain and suffering.

It is a process. Have faith. Have patience. And continue the work. For you are doing quite well with this process. We would pause for a moment of healing now.

Question: I have one. It is sort of an addendum to the last question and the response. GOD's own timing is fine with me. But just out of curiosity, what are the chances of accomplishing this shift of consciousness within, say, this lifetime?

MASTERS: The chances are good that would occur. You see, from our perspective where we see the eons and eons of suffering, denigration and pain that your soul has experienced, we see you on the one-yard line. You see the one-yard line as a mile long. It is a difference in perspective. So we would affirm to you that the reason that you are here is that you have evolved yourself in a way, and to a degree, that is quite probable that you will move through the blockages that you have not yet moved through in your consciousness. So we would say that the chances are good.

What you must remember, and what you are being protected from, is the following: At this point, you believe that growth must be accompanied by pain. Although you are desirous of growth, you are not desirous of pain. Yet you believe that growth comes with pain in a portion of your consciousness. So you still have a subconscious desire to create pain in order to know that you are growing.

We are working with you to develop a new truth. That truth is that growth does not have to be accompanied by pain. Growth can come in a wonderfully, beautifully effortless way, and that your lessons can be innocuous, if you choose. You are accepting this more and more, little by little. And as you accept this more and more, you will be able to experience more growth. For you will no longer associate growth with pain, and therefore send out the conflicting energy that you do not want pain, and therefore you do not want growth. Do you understand this?

Comment: Yeah. It hits home pretty well. Thank you.

MASTERS: You are very welcome. So again, see things, if you can, from our perspective, where you are on the one-yard line. You do not have a marathon to run.

Comment: I just have to hold onto the ball!

MASTERS: The ball is **within** you! It is the light of GOD that **is** you. You cannot drop this ball. Do you feel what is coming to you now?

Comment: Yes.

Question: My question ties into a couple of other questions, part of which is responsibility for a situation. I've been working with the tape of the session from two weeks ago. And one of the phrases, I believe that is on that tape is, "as above, so below." And I look at the below, and I wonder what on earth is above. But somehow there's something wrong with the logic there, I think. That just because "A" equals "B", doesn't mean that all "B" equals "A." And then one of the affirmations given to me was "I cannot suffer." And when I am feeling pain, and rotten and exhausted, then I wonder what on earth that means.

MASTERS: We would work with these questions. We would clarify what is meant by "as above, so below."

You see, existence for you actually occurs on many levels. The physical existence, which seems to be the lion's share of most humans' reality, is but one level. That is what is referred to as the "so below." It is referred to as "so below" because it occurs in a space where vibrations are slowed. Therefore vibrations are lower than they are in our realm of existence, where vibrations are speeded.

What we meant by that phrase was that the spiritual essence, or consciousness, of the individual dictates the experiences on the earth plane. As above (as in spirit), so below (as in flesh). And as the spiritual consciousness evolves, the earth plane experiences evolve, or shall we say in your case, dissolve. "Love cannot suffer" (which is an extremely powerful affirmation) helps to counteract deep beliefs that are held in your soul's consciousness (as above) that there is a price to be paid, or there must be a suffering in repentance for things that have been experienced in the past.

You are moving out of the consciousness where you believe, on the level of your soul (as above) that there must be a price to be paid, and there must be suffering for atonement for events that occurred in the dimmer portions of your soul's experience and expression.

As that consciousness shifts, your earthly existence will shift. For you will no longer believe, and therefore no longer create, experiences of suffering. As you continually tell yourself love will not suffer, what you tell yourself is that you are choosing to identify, and you are choosing to believe, and therefore you are choosing to **be** that part of you which is only unconditional love.

Unconditional love does not know suffering. So you are choosing that path, and you are moving yourself out of the realm where you can create suffering for yourself. You are transforming your mind so that you no longer believe that you must create suffering in order to have peace, or oneness, with GOD. So you are healing in your spiritual self (as above) and, therefore your physical self (so below). Does this clarify it for you?

Comment: Somewhat. I feel as though I really don't know what the next step is in clearing up things.

MASTERS: The next step is also the first step, and that is surrender. You are taking many actions on the physical plane, and you are taking many actions on the spiritual plane. Your next step is the first step, and that is to surrender. You may work with this prayer, and we will expand the range of this prayer so that it has relevance to everyone.

Mother/Father GOD, I surrender my will to Thy will. Thy will is for me to have peace. This will is for me to have joy. Thy will is for me to have abundance. Thy will is for me to have Light. Therefore I open myself to Thy will. I ask you to transform me. I ask you to transform my mind. I ask you to transform my body. I ask you to transform my affairs. So that my will is Thy will. Thy will be done. AMEN.

Individually, you must know that you do not have to create suffering in order to experience growth. There is no price to be paid. You may forgive yourself on a deeper level of those things that you know, and those things that you do not know. For you are innocent. You are perfect. At any given time in your soul's evolution, you did the best that you could with where you were. You are constantly recreating yourself. With every breath, you choose to view and believe yourself anew. And with every breath, you choose to view and believe that you are more and more aligned with the consciousness of GOD. **GOD cannot suffer**. Blessings to you. Love **will not** suffer. GOD is love.

Question: What is the meaning of the word "Amen?"

MASTERS: Amen is an incantation. Most simply put, it is an acknowledgment of the oneness of all things...the infinity and power of GOD. Acknowledging the oneness of all things, and the infinity and power of GOD invokes the infinity and power of GOD into the situation that is being "amen-ed."

Question: A quick question regarding that. This may seem like an evil question, but I'm going to ask it anyhow. Do you hear me in the mornings when I invoke my Amens in the bus on the way to work? Are you there?

MASTERS: My dear, we are always with you. For **you** are always with **us**. You see, there is no separation, except the separation that you perceive and create. But you are moving in a different way. You are opening and removing the veils that you believe separate us. You know of our presence in every aspect of your life. You are invoking our presence and the presence of Infinite Light in every aspect of your life.

For the group, it is important, once again, to understand that we are not here only for a specific portion, or aspect, of your human existence. As you invoke the power of Light in every aspect of your life...in your sexuality, in your business, in your family affairs, in your "all," then you experience the abundance and fullness of Light, as it has always been available to you. It has never been separated from any part of your expression. For **all** is Light.

We will conclude with this prayer and this healing:

Mother/Father GOD, I open to the light within me more, and more, and more with every breath, with every thought, and with every action. I give this light permission to permeate every aspect of my being. I understand that this light is not separated from any aspect of my expression. I understand that I am not separated from any aspect of this light. I understand that all is light. I understand that all is power. I understand that all is abundance. I understand that all is peace. I understand that I am a part of this all. I have all these qualities as well. And as I invoke them, and acknowledge them, they become more real and apparent to me. I remove the illusion that these things are withheld from me. I remove the illusion that your energy is separate from me. I remove the illusion that your energy is separate from me. For your energy is me. AMEN.

CHAPTER 4.
YOUR DIVINE NATURE

Greetings to all the creations of GOD's Light who are here. It is our pleasure and our honor to serve you tonight in this way. And we thank you once again for the courage that you exhibit by moving forward along your path of light.

We will talk to you tonight about your path of Light. For each of you has been placed squarely on the path that your soul has decided upon, in agreement with the universe, prior to this incarnation. As you have navigated through a portion of this incarnation, your path, and the specifics of your path, have also been constructed in a wonderful way. And we are continuing to guide you in this process. Se we thank you for the courage that you exhibit, and we acknowledge the courage that you exhibit in moving down your path.

We would underline, first of all, that your path begins within. You have all, to some degree, done work with yourselves to nurture the Light that lives within you as your life force, and to grow that light, to cultivate that Light, so that it subsumes your being....so that your consciousness is **only** of Light, and your physical expression **exudes** only that Light. The codings of your soul then merge with your human consciousness while in body. This is the way of the Christ. This is the process of becoming Christ-ed, and this is an experience that is open to each and every one you, and that during the course of this lifetime, you will experience to a large degree. We would ask you to take a moment, however, and reflect on that statement. You are becoming Christ-ed. You are becoming **of** the Christ. You might examine your reactions to this statement. You might examine the codings that are a part of your psychological makeup that are unleashed when you hear those words, your reaction to those words, what those words connote to you. Take one more moment and examine that.

You see, those words are loaded for many of you. They bring back memories of your experience in traditional earth religions, and they bring to you a memory of separation -- where you believed that there was a separate, supreme being who was **the** Christ. And it would be heresy to, in any way, to believe that you, as a lowly and undeserving human being, could imagine that **you** were part of **the Christ**. We would tell you, of course, that this is an error of your thinking, for we are teaching you a new way.

As you recall, we talked about who and what GOD is, and who and what GOD is not. We will tonight review who and what is the Christ consciousness. And this relates very much to your path, and the path you have opened to. For you have all opened, to some degree, to the path of Christ-edness. The energy of the being that you know as Jesus Christ, who walked the earth some 2,000 years ago, was an energy not unlike yours. It was a human energy. However, this human energy never forgot his connection with the Creator...the Source. This human energy manifested with that connection, and taught using that connection, and **lived** with that connection, and continually expanded that connection just as you are doing.

That individual reached a Christ-ed state where his auric field was so open to the energy of GOD, and was vibrating in such harmony with the energy of GOD, and vibrating in such fullness of GOD, that there was not any perception of separation between his energy and the energy of GOD. That is a path that is open on the earth to many. For there is enough Light to help to expand the energy field of each individual, so that it opens in a more full and effortless way to all the energy of GOD. And it does so without imbalance of disruption, for there is enough Light to support this transformation now. So your energy is not unlike the energy of Christ. Any part of your consciousness that believes that it is not worthy of this manifestation of life is in error. And we would call out that error to you now. For part of your soul's path was to learn of the error, and move through the error of your thinking, and accept your divinity...your Christ-edness...yourselves.

So who is Christ-ed? **You** contain within your energy as you continue to nurture it **all** the abilities...wisdom...of Christ, the energy of GOD in man. Do not be afraid of this. Know that your path is opening in a wonderful way, and know that we are guiding you in a very deep way to help you navigate through your human existence and commune more and more with the Divine that lives within you, and merges with you. As this Divine energy merges with you more and more, your life becomes effortless. Your life's path becomes effortless. And the true purpose of your existence becomes more and more clear. This will unfold for each of you in your own way over the next several years.

Know also that what you are doing is magnetizing yourself from inside, so that you are vibrating only with the Light of GOD. As this occurs, you attract to you only that which is a reflection of the Light of GOD. You begin more and more to attract to you only that which is abundant. You begin to attract only that which is loving. You become more and more able to attract to you **only** that which is full, and fulfilled, and joyous, and expansive and positive.

Know that this process within is then reflected in your outer world. This is very important. For **all** that you see in your outer world is a reflection of your inner consciousness. So as your consciousness moves into a Christ-ed realm, as your consciousness moves into the consciousness of GOD while embodied, which is the Christ-ed realm, you then draw to you all those wonderful things. And it begins within, in your work with yourself. So we congratulate you on the work that you have done. We congratulate you on the work that you are doing. We congratulate you on the work that you **will** do. For you make the space for the Light of GOD to live more fully and more deeply within you.

Each of you, as you move forward, as you evolve in this lifetime, will have some element of service to the Light as a central focus for your lives. For in serving the Light, you nurture and grow the Light on the earth. And this is important because your task collectively has been to work with Light while on earth, and to activate the Light centers within others simply by your mere presence as you expand the Light that lives within you. And through service, you consciously work with the Light of others, and you consciously touch the Light of others, and a chain reaction occurs. As a result, the earth heals, and the inhabitants of the earth heal, and the earth is evolved into its next phase of existence. Many of you have questions about how this would affect the earth, the "earth changes".

We would not deny that the earth is changing. We would, however, attempt to minimize any concerns that you might have, or any fears you might feel about this. For the cataclysmic events that have been foretold many times have, to a large degree, been mitigated by the amount of Light that is now resident on the earth. Individuals like you are largely responsible for anchoring the Light on the earth that helps to minimize the possible effects of earth changes. So we would say to you, remove from your energy field your fear of your own power, your fear of your own Christ-edness, and any misperceptions and preconceived notions of the energy of the Christ that no longer serve you.

We would suggest that you also consciously remove your fear of earth changes. For as you remove any fear from your energy field, you cannot draw to you that which is reflective of that fear. For it is no longer a part of you. It is no longer a part of your core magnetism. And this enables you to move down your life's path in a more effortless way, unimpeded by fears, conscious or subconscious. Be not afraid of the words that we offer to you. Be not afraid of the concept of yourself as a Christ-ed and powerful being. Be not afraid of subconscious memories that you may hold of prior existence where you have not used your power for the greatest good of all, and not used your Light for the greatest good of all. For we are working with each of you individually to blot out any subconscious memories that you have of the past that would impede you from your current progress, and from your future probabilities on this plane. That is the grace of GOD which you invoke, and that we bring to you from the heart of GOD as you call upon us.

There are some who are uncomfortable with this information, for it may seem radical. And it certainly is radical when compared to the orthodox teachings of your traditional religions. But as you know, we are bringing you truth in an undistorted way. So we would say to you, "Be not afraid." And we now have a very special guest who works with you and teaches through this being.

ൟൟൟൟ

Greetings from the Heart of GOD. I come to you today in this way to say that which I have done, you shall also do. When I walked the earth, and after my tour of duty on the earth, I left many teachings. Some of those teachings have been misused and distorted, and you carry within your consciousness memories and fears based on these distortions. And my truth has reemerged through other sources....through my book, "A Course In Miracles," and through channels who have been open to my Light. And my teachings in truth are converging. Just as I am able, through the many channels that are open to me now, to make a deeper contact with you on the earth plane, and to work more closely with you in every way.

I have power because you give me power. And what I mean by that is, in your consciousness you look to me as the being who has the power to transform you and create miracles. I would step down from that pedestal now. For I support you. However, the truth is that you invoke the power to transform yourself from your own being...from your own soul. I support you. I facilitate this process. You hold that power. That which I have done, you will also do. Yet you will do greater things as you understand this more deeply, and as you release your fear, which is based on old and erroneous teachings

of your own Christ-ed nature. The healing that will take place through you will be nothing short of miraculous. The shifts in the consciousness of others that will take place through you will be nothing short of miraculous. And the bliss that you will feel, and that you will continue to feel as you, too, come in full union with our Creator, will be nothing short of miraculous.

Be not afraid. For this is what you have chosen. Be not afraid, for I, and many, help you. All that you must do is call on us. And you may call on me by my name. You know it as Jesus. Pause for a moment. Feel the energy of transformation as it moves through you.

~~~~~~~~

We would thank you for your attentiveness during this portion of this session. We have covered a topic that is both wide and deep, and you can refer to your notes and you can read the words, but most importantly, **feel** the energy of transformation that is encoded in the words.

Many of you also ask if things are going to get better, why do they seem to get worse now. What you are doing is moving out all illusions, and some facets of your human life are based on illusion. That situation is not unlike a house that is built on a foundation of quicksand. So you feel shifts occurring in your life. You feel uncertainties and movements in occurring within your lives. This is to show you what is real and what is illusion. You are learning more and more to discern what is in truth and what is illusion, and you have opened to this. That which is an illusion shall fall away. Not in any way that would cause you harm or hardship, for that is not the intent, but in a way that will reveal only that which is truth.

All is in Divine order. As above, so below. We are thrilled with the progress you have made. For you have certainly
~~~~~~~~

taken to heart the words and energies that have been made available to you. And this, of course, is no surprise for you have asked for this. Each and every one of you has asked for the healing, for the power, for the insights and for the growth that has been made available to you. We are thrilled to work with this specific group this evening, and we begin this evening's discussion with the truth that all is in Divine order. Because all who are needing to be here today are here. You see, you are embarking on a path where you live your light, where you accept your light, where your light ceases to be a theoretical concept or a religious or spiritual construct that is reserved for your most private musings. Your light is instead an integral part of **who you are**. It actually subsumes the part of you that is illusion. This is the path for each of you. This is what you have desired. This is the Divine plan for your lives. So we are thrilled to offer you the encouragement to live your light. We will elaborate on what that means.

The first thing it means, of course, is to always remember *only* who you are. As you know, many times you have been conditioned to define yourselves by your limitations. You have been taught to define yourselves by your lack. You have been taught to define yourselves by your shortcomings. You have been taught to define yourselves by the parameters of the illusion. We would say to you that the parameters of the illusion are no longer holding for you because you are choosing not to live in the illusion any more. You are, instead, choosing to live in the Light of GOD.

The first step in living your light is constantly remembering who you are. You may begin this process quite simply by observing your reaction to stimuli in your world. Your experiences are your teachers. They show you where you are aligned with the Light of GOD, and living with the Light of GOD, and where you are not.

With each experience that you have, we would suggest that you examine the experience, and examine your reaction to the experience. Ask your self, "How would the innocent, perfect, powerful, peaceful, full child of GOD react to this situation?" And by asking yourself that question, you begin to react in that way. Do not react in denial. For you, of course, make note of the emotional charge and the need for emotional release*, and you do so. But you begin to continually "yank" yourself back into the framework of Heaven. You continually "yank" yourself back to the realm of infinite consciousness. You continue to elevate your thoughts, you vibration, your very being. You continually elevate it to the place where it knows no denigration, or limitation, or lack, or suffering, or pain, or difficulty, or doubt. So your first step is to react to every situation as if you are the beloved innocent, perfect, full, beautiful, capable, powerful child of GOD. For you are!

*Author's Comments

The process described here is the process of Emotional Release, which will be covered more fully in Chapter 7, Transforming Your Consciousness. Emotional Release is a key part of your spiritual transformation. The "Emotional Release Process" is also outlined fully in the Author's previous book ***"Pathways to Inner Peace": Lifesaving Processes for Healing Heart, Mind and Soul***.

Know also, that your Father is always with you. A practical exercise in this is using the power of your imagination to see yourself differently. You can see yourself as a child who has a rich and powerful Father. You can see yourself as a child who has a wonderfully affirming Father. You can see yourself as a child who has a generous and beneficent Father. As you play this role of the child who has such a wonderful Father, how can you then lack confidence? How then can you lack strength? How then can you lack vision and resolve? For your Father is always with you. And your Father has infinite power, infinite wealth and infinite love. And so do you.

This understanding helps you to live your light. You may also continually invoke the Light of GOD. With every breath, you may program your mind to inhale more of the light of GOD and expand the Light of GOD that lives within you. Through your affirmations, you may continually tell yourself, and condition yourself that, **With every breath, I invoke the Light of GOD. With every breath I expand in my light. With every breath I am my light.**" Thus you may allow the Light of GOD to transform you in a deeper and deeper way.

We would suggest that you breathe now and avail yourselves to the healing energy that we offer to you at this time.

~~~

You may also live your light by not letting others define you. You may live your light by not giving others power over you to determine your sense of self, or your sense of worth, or your sense of self worth. You may live your light by not giving outer the power to make you feel one way or another. Instead, you live your light by feeling that you are protected, that you are guided, that you are supported, that you are embraced, that you are on a path that is wonderful, and mystical, and full of adventure, and excitement, and joy, and bliss. You will float over any obstacle that you perceive, because any obstacle is simply a creation of your imagination, and it is used to simply show fear so that fear may be eradicated.

So you see, as you become more and more light, you live more and more within the parameters of light, and outside the parameters of the mass human consciousness, which is the consciousness of pain and suffering. And we would let you
~~~

know unequivocally that you have support. You have our support. You have the support of each other. You have the support of this physical Temple of Light that you have built for your soul. We thank you in a very deep way for the courage that you exhibit in choosing to move forward in your light. Know that light will always be there to expand you. And know that you are that light. Breathe and feel our healing energies.

Your Divine Intuition (Channeling Light)

This subject is quite innocuous. We will talk about the art and science of channeling, for that is an interest that you all have consciously or subconsciously. We will talk about the role of channeling in the process of spiritual growth and development. We will talk about the ultimate purpose of your being in body now, and we will then answer your questions about this process. And we will answer any additional questions that you have.

We would begin by affirming and reassuring you that you too have the ability to channel. We would begin drawing for you a picture of continuous energy. Where all is energy, and all energy is intertwined. Hold in your mind, if you will, a vision of the union of the universe where all is one – and one is all. Different aspects of the "all" vibrate at different rates; and, therefore, have different densities. Different aspects of the "all" absorb and dispense light in different ways; and therefore, have different colors. Different aspects of the "all" have different relative qualities and combinations of qualities and therefore appear differently, but "all" is one. That is the truth.

Imagine if you will, that activities are also a part of this continuum. The ingestion, the use and the dispersion of light is a part of this process. Several times we have alluded to the absorption of light and the dispersion of light. Well, you see, light comes in many forms. Sometimes it comes in the form of snippets of information that you receive from another realm of existence. As you are able to absorb more light, it may come in the form of voices that you may hear briefly. As your energy field can hold even more light, the light may come in the form of sustained contact or overshadowing of your consciousness by the consciousness of a being of light. These are all on a continuum. They are all part of the same process, the process of absorption and dispersion of light.

We would offer an analogy. You have a phone line, and you have a fax machine. Sometimes that wire transmits a voice (when it is used for a phone) and sometimes that wire transmits data (when it is used as a fax machine). The voice and the data have some of the same qualities, but differ with respect to the electromagnetic charge. By the same token (and this is not new to some of you) the energy that flows through you does so naturally all the time. That is why we many times say that channeling is simply the ingestion, absorption and expulsion of this light as information. As you expand your energy field, you are able to sustain more light. The more light you are able to sustain, the more information you are able to sustain. The more information you are able to sustain, the more information you are able to disburse through the process of flow. At some point along this continuum (for again, understanding the unity of energy and the unity of the universe) you are able to sustain enough light to support a being of light merging with your consciousness. And this is channeling. However, getting a brief snippet of information is channeling to some degree. Stream of Consciousness Writing (sometimes called channeled writing) is just that. It is channeling to some degree. Giving readings is channeling to some degree. It is all on that continuum.

The analogy that we would draw to you regarding channeling is very simple. When there is a pregnancy, the body has another being that starts growing, and growing, and growing. And it grows to the point where it becomes an independent life force that can be sustained within the sponsoring life force. Think of channeling as growing the energy to the point where your energy field can sustain or sponsor the fullness of another entity or group of entities of light within you light field or your auric consciousness. So think of channeling as opening yourself, or expanding yourself to the point where you can sustain another light in the same way that a woman's body expands to accommodate another life force.

We would also extend this analogy, because as a woman moves through pregnancy, the body prepares itself for the task:

more food must be eaten. The analogy here is that in order to move down a path of channeling, more light must be ingested, for more energy is required. And the light – just as the woman's body changes to accommodate the growing independent life force, the subtle changes in the body's chemistry must occur: hormonal levels shift, etc. in pregnancy. I believe you are all aware of these changes.

By that same token, the energy of the host, when channeling, also acts on the body to change aspects of the central nervous system, the motor responses, the vocal cords, etc. In channeling, the body is literally retrofitted to sustain, or host, another light form. So, we could conclude this portion of the discussion by once again reassuring you that channeling is an easy task to accomplish. We would then segue into spiritual growth and development. The way that we would segue into spiritual growth and development is by looking at the purpose of such growth.

Spiritual Growth and Development

The purpose of such growth is to expand the light which lives within each of you. The purpose is to become more and more familiar with this light and understand its true origin, which is the source of all, the all, or GOD. By nurturing this light, understanding its perfection, its infinity, its power, its peace, its passion, its connection – by doing all of this, you then understand GOD. For you understand the GOD force that lives within each of you. As you understand this, you live more in accordance with this GOD-force, and you expand this GOD force not only within yourselves, but also within others. For it ignites the GOD force in others. This GOD force evolves you and others to what you were meant to be -- reflections of GOD's light and energy. You then complete the task on earth, which is your transformation and your creation on the earth plane of all that you hold in your mind. For you then manifest fully in the GOD-self form and you evolve yourself fully. As you do this, you then prepare to return to the source, for you understand who you truly are. You align yourself with that source and you return to it. That is the purpose of spiritual growth.

The by-products of this purpose include the ability to channel, and other capabilities that are the result of the merging of your soul, or your higher energy, or your eternal self, or your GOD-self with your human self. These by-products of your evolution are very natural, and should not scare you. We would say that the most loving purpose of learning to channel is the fulfillment of the desire to bond with, and attract, and grow with guidance, nurturing, healing, and support of other beings that you can accommodate through your channel as it grows. The purpose is also to understand how you can love yourself more completely and unconditionally. For as you move your human self into alignment with unconditional love, that is of course how you ascend. There are some who might equate the ability to channel with being lovable. We would say that being lovable comes first, and learning to channel is a by-product of understanding your lovability – of living and being in accordance with GOD's unconditional love. There is a difference. We would simply make you aware of that difference, so that your desire stems not from the ego or the ego's desire to feel lovable, or acceptable, or superior to others, but so that your desire manifests from the heart. From the true desire of your soul to expand and merge with your human consciousness and be your human consciousness, and vice versa. So the process of growth and development is simply the process of opening your channel to more and more light through prayer, meditation, emotional release, and the transformation that occurs when these things are used in combination. And we will support you in your efforts to do this. This is what we would say about spiritual growth and development at this time. There is, of course, much, much more. But for now, we would open this session to questions before we move forward.

Question:: I am interested in what you said early on about light being received as snippets of information, or as voices. This seems to me a mechanism of intuition. I am very interested in intuition and was wondering if you could elaborate on that.

MASTERS: Yes we will. You are absolutely correct in that this issue is a mechanism of intuition. You see, the human consciousness has developed many defenses and preoccupations that keep your human consciousness from living fully with awareness of our realm of existence. Part of the reason for this veil between the worlds is for you so that you are not distracted from the events of your world in such a way that it would threaten your survival. For example in earlier incarnations, humans did not have the natural defenses of claws, fangs, or strength or the natural protection of fur. The human form had to use intelligence and wit to survive and had to be quite diligently alert to all "earthly" information (such as when a human was being stalked by a wild animal). As a result, humans could not become too distracted by living simultaneously in two realms of existence. If the human form became too distracted, the human form would not survive.

We would give you examples from the consciousness of the channel, who spent one lifetime channeling light from the divine to the earth plane in such an intense way that the channel did not take nourishment from the earth. The channel starved to death. The protection mechanism of the veil was established in a stronger and stronger way so that the human could concentrate on the physical world. The protection mechanism in these current times is the protection mechanism that the child adopts as the child matures, so that the child can navigate in a way that is consistent with the mass consciousness. The child literally closes the veil as it evolves. The child is told "you cannot see other beings – you cannot hear other beings, and your imaginary playmate is not real". The child then believes it and the veil is closed. Where, in truth, the child is simultaneously present in the earth world and in other worlds. But the child loses that connection so that the child would protect itself and not be labeled schizophrenic. So we say all of this to say that there is a veil that has been created by your consciousness.

There are times where we can break through that veil. Many times when your consciousness is very relaxed, or very focused on a task, your defenses are down. Small pieces of information can slip through and inspire you, or make you curious. Other times you may perceive flashes of light, which are indications that you are seeing through your world, and seeing glimpses of other worlds. Other things that you may find occurring are that you may find your consciousness in some other time.

For example, you may find yourself in a situation that you found yourself in weeks, months, years, or decades ago. You realize that your consciousness is in a different space (somewhat like a daydream, but a more vivid daydream) and you bring your consciousness back to the present where your physical body is. What this is, is the expansion for a brief moment of yourself into your multi-dimensional self, which exists on many dimensions. And this, too, is a function of the momentary opening that occurs when the defenses are down.

The process of prayer and meditation, which facilitates spiritual growth, and thus your intuition, is a process of habitually depriving the outer senses. When you deprive the outer senses, you strengthen the inner senses, so that your ability to navigate on our realm becomes strengthened through deliberate practice and the deliberate focus of your consciousness on **our** world versus **your** world. This facilitates the process which is one of many reasons why prayer and meditation is vital to spiritual growth.

Using Your Divine Nature to Create Your Prosperity

It is our pleasure and our honor once again to serve you in this way. We notice always the changing dynamics of the group, and we put together a program that is for the highest good of all. We thank you for participating in this effort, and you must thank yourselves for opening in this way to the information that leads you towards the light that you already are. We say that to emphasize the truth that the light of GOD lives within each of you. Your task now is not to connect with GOD as you perceive GOD outside of you, but to connect with the light of GOD that lives within you and to grow that light within you, and nurture it, and bring it into alignment with that portion of the light of GOD that you perceive outside of you. We qualify that by saying that you perceive it outside of you, however it truly is a part of all you are creating, individually and in mass.

We would talk to you tonight very briefly about the nature of creation, and the creation of the experiences that you are having in this life, at this time, both individually and in mass. We will keep this portion of the talk brief, because we do understand that there are many questions on this topic that have yet to be asked.

You must first understand the nature of creating a situation. Imagine if you will, a committee. This committee is chaired by your higher self, or your soul. There are other beings of light on this committee who love you and have a vested interest in the event that is created. The other committee members may consist of other souls (or higher selves of others) who might be participants in the event on the earth plane, as well as guides and teachers who are working with you and/or others at any given time. These beings, of course, are tapped into the Infinite Intelligence. In a sense, they do complex mathematical calculations of probabilities to choose or select events that would be for the greatest good of all. There is no way to really convey what truly goes on in these planning sessions, except to bring into your mind pictures that you will understand such as the understanding that you have a committee and its functions. The committee discusses potential courses of action and feeds the courses of action into the equivalent of a large Cray super computer, which would do many models and simulations of events to assess probable outcomes. This occurs, and the committee agrees on a course of events on the earth plane. The place where this occurs is a space in the world of reality which can best be described as the plane of creativity, a plane of existence that is a mental plane.

This plane is not a true physical or spatial condition. On this mental plane, events and occurrences are planned, and modeled, and trialed prior to their existence on the earth plane. This plane of creativity, of course, is a plane where light exists, and where events are speeded up so that many simulation models can be observed before a conclusion is reached. And then, once the event has been formed or created it the perfect way on this plane of creativity, the vibrational energy of the event is slowed down and then placed on the earth plane. As a result, those probabilities occur.

We would go on to the purpose of this planning committee. Their purpose is to ensure that the events chosen are for the greatest good of all. To teach all who are involved the lesson that is needing to be learned at that time. And the participants, on the level of their higher selves, have agreed to this. And then the event occurs. It is a teaching and a learning experience for all who are involved. This is not only based on your thoughts and your beliefs, but also on the level of your higher self. You have chosen events that would teach you the lessons that you need to learn at any given point in time.

You do not have to take a comprehensive inventory, of your issues. The events in your life will ensure that the things that you must learn are learned in a way that is for your greatest good. So we have just described how this process works, with a little more detail, and we do this to encourage you to look at the events that occur in a new light.

Do not judge them as evidence of your inherent "badness," or your inherent disconnection from the light. Do not give these events that are your teachers any negative or unaffirming meanings. They are simply the perfect tools at any given time that you are using to realign every aspect of your consciousness to the light. This goes back to not judging any part of your consciousness as being inferior, or unevolved, or anything that would cause it to be less than what it is. For it is all of GOD, and it is all perfect. For it works in a perfect way to bring all of you in alignment with GOD's consciousness.

So please be confident and comfortable in looking at your life situations, and in asking what you are to learn from them so that you can be free to no longer create situations that are unaffirming. You can receive the same lesson from an affirming, and easy, and beautiful experience. So which do you choose? We would suggest that you choose to see you lessons and teachings in a wonderfully loving and affirming way. And you may do so first of all by understanding that, although in the past you may have created lessons through pain and suffering, the past has no power over you, and you now create your lessons in a wonderful way.

For example, in an earlier part of your life, you may have believed that you were unlovable and therefore, undeserving of love. Perhaps you believed this because you were bombarded by messages from the mass consciousness that said that if you did not fit a certain standard of perfection, you could not have your hearts desires. Perhaps you believed these messages subconsciously and began to create your outer world based on the "untruth" of these messages. Perhaps you then created a "love situation" where your partner was unable to love you in the ways that you wanted or needed to be loved. This situation probably caused you endless anguish and pain. Eventually, you learn that you must first love yourself and when you do, others will reflect this love back to you. As you learn this lesson, you are then able to attract a partner that reflects your growing love for self back to you. As you attract a more affirming partner, you demonstrate the lesson you need to learn in a wonderful and affirming way.

So now you see how you create lessons for yourself on an individual level. On the mass level lessons are created in the same way. To gauge the level of mass consciousness, and where mass consciousness must be healed, the large committees meet. The large committees have been meeting for many, many eons to determine mass events, and then the mass events occur. However, **all participants in mass events are willing participants**.

We will give you an example: The event that occurred in your city of Oklahoma several years ago. In that event there was a small infant who was photographed in the arms of a rescue worker. This photograph was seen by many, many millions of eyes around the globe. It covered several national news magazines, and this image was repeatedly seen not only in print, but through all forms of mass communication. And this image of this infant in the arms of the rescue worker became the symbol for this event.

So this event was truly a lesson for humanity. For this picture, this symbol, an "innocent victim," an "innocent child," murdered as the result of hatred, misunderstanding, distrust, taught millions and millions and millions a lesson in love. This "innocent victim" was a volunteer who volunteered on the level of the soul to teach a lesson to millions of humans about love. So this volunteer chose to be involved in this event in a very prominent way to teach this lesson. We do not say that this volunteer was not innocent, nor do we say that this volunteer was not a victim, we simply say that as you train yourselves to see events as events in a new way, you no longer have to judge the events with the human yardstick that would obscure the lesson. We, of course, always advocate having compassion for others. We, too, have the utmost compassion for these situations. We have a responsibility to help you to see the situations more clearly, and more objectively, for the lessons that they offer. For that is the true reason that the situations have occurred both within your individual lives, and within your collective consciousness.

We will continue with any questions that you might have at this time, and please do not be shy. For we have seen some of the questions that you would like to ask, and we have prepared responses.

Question: How is that little child with the rescue worker a sign of love? Is that in the sense that she gave her life for our lesson? Could you explain a little bit?

MASTERS: Yes. Certainly. We would explain that by first framing it in the context of existence on the earth plane. We would use the symbol of a theater. The earth plane is a theater where aspects of consciousness are examined as if these aspects of consciousness are players on a stage. The higher selves, or souls, of all the players are sitting in the audience observing this drama in an objective way. For they know that the play is only two hours out of an infinite life. Therefore, with this scene in your mind, you see that a two-hour play, in the broader infinity of life, does not seem like that much of a substantial part. But of course, if you are a character in the play, and if you are centered in that character, it may seem like everything, for it is the basis of your perception.

In this situation the child was an actor in this drama that enabled the world to see the horrible, horrible consequences that could occur when there is not love. We would say "horrible" consequences, for they seem like horrible consequences from the perspective of the human psyche, and they are truly destructive consequences. So this child, in volunteering for this role, taught people the following lesson, almost as if the child stood on a stage and recited the following words: "Do you now see how destructive hatred can be? Do you now see how sacred life is, and that it should not be treated cavalierly in this way? Do you now see what the consciousness of hatred has created? And do you want to move forward in that consciousness? Or do you want to shift that consciousness towards a consciousness that is affirming, and loving and of light?" So if those were the words this child would say while this child was on the stage in this drama, those words would be an act of love. Those words lovingly taught others to seek love. For the consciousness of hatred can be destructive. On some level, the consciousness of many shifted as a result of this act.

Question: Did she choose to play that role before she came to earth?

MASTERS: Yes. In the example that we gave where there are planning committee meetings, there are individual smaller group meetings for small events. There are extremely large planning committee meetings for extremely large events. All the souls who are involved in the large events play some role in the planning committee meetings.

Question: I like what you said about choosing affirming experiences that are our lesson learned. Choosing lessons that are affirming. Can spirit give some examples of that, or talk about that a little bit more?

MASTERS: Yes. What you have done tonight is you have opened to a shift in your perception. When we worked with you in healing energy, you accepted the healing energy that said that you would continue shifting your consciousness to create lessons in wonderfully affirming ways. For example, the truth is that GOD wants you to have everything, and would only give everything to you, but you must simply open to receive it.

There are two potential ways of learning this lesson. The first might be an experience that you would create that would cause you extreme lack and deprivation, and what would seem like misery, due to lack and deprivation. On the level of your soul, you would cry out to GOD to shift your consciousness, because this clearly does not seem as if it is consistent with the light, love and energy of GOD. That shift would occur, and eventually every aspect of your consciousness would accept a new principle, and would accept that truth of GOD, and the transformation would be complete. However this lesson would be learned through suffering.

We would instead suggest that you invoke the grace of GOD. The grace of GOD would immediately shift your perception to this new truth without your creation of what would seem to be terribly unaffirming events of deprivation and lack. You are moving on this path by simply being here and availing yourself of these truths when many choose not to.

We offer you many subtle and oblique lessons. There is a part of the collective consciousness that still envisions the energy of GOD as somber, angry and brooding. We bring you lessons of joy and mirth to help to shift that perception as well. We will illustrate by accessing the channel's consciousness to emphasize the point that we have just made.

When the channel first had tenants in his home, the tenants amassed many newspapers that had to be recycled. The channel lived in a house that is situated an appreciable distance from the curb, so getting the newspapers to the curb for recycling was a very difficult task. The newspapers would pile up quickly, and become very heavy. One morning the channel chose to punish himself by playing "beat the clock," where the channel raced against time. In this case the clock was beating the channel. So the channel chose to punish himself more by remembering that this was recycle day, and that the newspapers had to be transported to the street. And although they were not the channel's newspapers, nor his responsibility, they were a part of the channel's household. As the owner of the household, the channel chose this extra burden. The channel dragged these newspapers to the street, and sweated, and hurt his back. When the channel finished this task and returned to the garage, the channel then saw a red wagon that the tenants had placed there in order to carry the containers filled with newspapers up to the street.

The channel then learned the lesson that everything the channel needed was provided to the channel. But the channel chose to learn that lesson in a way that included some element of suffering so that the lesson would be deeply reinforced. In doing so, the channel learned another lesson, and that is that the channel did not have to incur the lessons through pain or suffering. The lesson could be incurred by simply opening his eyes to the truth, and continually asking that his eyes be opened to the truth. There are red wagons throughout your lives.

Question: Can you discuss divine order, and whether prayer, visualization and meditation affects the timing of events, the manifestation of events?

MASTERS: Yes. The planning committee is the example of divine order. The mass planning committee includes, of course, the source. Prayer, meditation, visualization and the like are ways of connecting with members and emissaries of the planning committee to exert more and more of your human desires onto that committee. As we said before, the committee creates many computer models of probable outcomes of events, as if the committee has a Cray supercomputer. When you conduct your visualizations and your prayers, you feed into those computer models. For you change the probabilities. For you consciously grow and change. Your efforts and your growth enable you to change the outcomes, at any given time through your invocation of the grace of GOD.

Question: So I take it than regarding prayer, actually what happens during the process of prayer is that you are connecting with the entities on the planning committee, is that correct? And thanking them on the work they have done on your behalf, but also requesting the manifestation of certain events or things. Is that what happens during the process of prayer?

MASTERS: Yes. We would say that prayer is simply an amplification of the request, and that amplification carries it forward and enables the planning committee to feed that data into the model. So when, through prayer, you send out information in a very, very strong powerful way. The request gets heeded, and worked on, and examined, and created in the context of everything that happens on this plane of creativity. Then you see the results. So prayer is taking action, and affirmative prayer helps the creative process, for it sends more energy to that creative process.

Question: In light of what the lesson is for this evening, I have a question on the employment situation I am going through right now. And I have had insight that probably, if I had not created this situation, I would not be sitting in this chair right now, so I guess I shouldn't judge it too much. But how do I go about getting out of this spiral of energy and move toward a more positive, not judgmental, a more affirming realization of the lessons that I need from this, and the abundance of lessons.

MASTERS: Yes. We are retrieving an answer for you from our "Cray" super computers. You see, once again, on the level of your soul, this is a temporary occurrence, and you are held very closely by your soul. For you have invoked, and merged your consciousness, with part of your soul's consciousness through this opening, and you have enabled more of your soul's infinite energy to be lodged in your energy field as a result of this opening.

Through this process, you are learning the art of "**non substitution**". Many times you substitute the synthetic light of the false-ego for the light of GOD. You believe that you get light from those things such as your job title, income, relationships, etc., as opposed to receiving light from GOD. For example you believe that your self-worth and well being comes from how the world views you, and you feel good about yourself only on the condition that the world treats you in a certain way, or blesses you with a certain job title or income. Your task now is to look only to GOD and not to the conduits through which your needs are supplied, for GOD is the ultimate supplier.

For example, you might visualize an infinite number of ways that your financial needs could be fulfilled. In a very practical sense, we would say that you release more fear of lack, not in an intellectual way, but in a visceral way, as you release this fear of lack, it has no power over you, and you can no longer create with it. So in your safe space, you may choose to repeat the following prayer:

Mother/Father GOD, I have fear. I fear that You would not support me. I fear that You would withhold from me. I fear that You would punish me for subconscious guilt that I feel. In my human mind I know this is error. I know now that You would not withhold from me. I know now that You would not punish me. I know now I need not feel guilt. Therefore, I ask You to change my perception. I ask that You take the fear, and I surrender it to You. I surrender it through my voice by expressing it. I surrender through my body by moving the fear through my body. I ask You to transform it so that I may create with expectancy that which I desire. I look not to people, places, or events for the satisfaction of my desires; I look only to You, who will work through an infinite number of people, places and events to ensure that I have what I need.

GOD sees not lack. GOD sees not need. GOD sees only the fullness and the infinity of all that GOD has created, including you. So when you see lack, you create it. When you see need, you create that situation of need. So when you see yourself only as GOD sees you, you move in alignment with GOD's vision of you, and your vision of yourself in truth. Through this process, you see yourself as full and complete. You already affirm, and truly believe, that you have everything. For you truly do. And as you change this belief, you open your perception more and more to receive everything. For you have already claimed it. You have already created it, and you truly already have it. So again, with that explanation, we would say that the best way to satisfy your need is to eliminate it. We are working with you now in healing. For we see that in several weeks you will have the things you desire. There is something, and we are giving the channel the vision of the sun rising on the horizon, for you. It will manifest in the next several weeks. Take comfort and solace in the light that surrounds you now. For it is your protector. It is your provider, and it is you. For it is the light of GOD that continually expands within you.

Question: I really enjoyed the story about the channel and the red wagon. I was laughing a lot. I was thinking about some of the situations that I was in, and it's funny to sit back and laugh at them. To see that everything was there, the red wagon. And I've been in that situation too. Where the wagon has been there, but I haven't seen it until much later. But I was wondering about the bigger issues that I've been creating for myself, and learning the hard way. And I very, very much want to learn things the easy way. I've tried meditations, visualizations, affirmations, prayers, all these things. I'm learning things the hard way still. I'm wondering , "Invoking the Grace of GOD," what does that mean? "I invoke the Grace of GOD" and that's all I have to say? I am really trying to learn this, but it takes me a long time, I guess, to learn anything. If you could say it again, I would appreciate it.

MASTERS: Our beautiful flower. We are sending healing energy to you now. You see, there are many, many aspects of consciousness. You have received millions, if not billions, of subtle messages that would tell you that life is to be suffered through. You have heard that the only way to gain is through pain. Many of these messages have lodged in your consciousness.

You also carry with you a belief in karma and that it is your karmic responsibility to complete tasks in a painful way that would give you lessons through pain. For you feel that "paying a karmic debt" is repentance. On a broad level, we would say that you can continually invoke the Grace of GOD, understanding that the Grace of GOD supersedes karma. Ask and invoke the Grace of GOD so that it touches every part of your consciousness, and repeatedly invite the Grace of GOD to touch, caress and transform every part of your consciousness so you no longer believe that lessons must be learned through pain and suffering.

This change in your perception heals your consciousness so that you no longer believe that you must pay karmic debts through pain and suffering. For you continually embrace the Grace of GOD.

On a more practical level, you may work with creative visualization. Visualize your present as if it were exactly how you want it to be. Visualize your future exactly as you want it to be, without obstacles, without the painful, seemingly unpleasant situations where you would feel trapped now. You can move forward, and affirmatively create your present and your future, without memories of past suffering, but with glorious visions of future joy, and glorious experiences of the current joy that you experience through prayer and meditation. Then you literally erase the ability to create unaffirming events.

You also erase the ability to create unaffirming events by taking the sting out of them by understanding they really have no meaning. By seeing it more objectively from the perspective of your higher self, as part of the theater audience as opposed to being the player on the stage. This of course, is easier said than done, or so it seems. But as you become more comfortable in prayer and meditation, you become very adept at seeing the world through the prism of your higher self. And this, too, helps you.

Question: With the question asked earlier, and the question I asked before, I feel it takes a long time for things to manifest. I feel that I've been asking for some of the same things all of my life, and they haven't manifested. And I wonder if it's not just part of some cosmic plan, or if I'm not doing it correctly, or why am I not getting the kind of manifestation that I was looking for.

MASTERS: This is a very complex question. And we have formulated a very complex answer, so we ask you for patience and forbearance. We would say first of all that you are doing wonderfully in your process of removing blockages to receiving that which you desire in every aspect of your life. You have embraced, to some extent, the concept of emotional release which clears your energy field of blockages. You have enhanced your awareness of the presence of GOD through prayer and meditation. And you have continually opened your channel to light through other spiritual and mystic disciplines that you have pursued. And we applaud you and support you in this. So you are doing all the right things. And so you are saying, "Yes I am doing all the right things, so why am I still frustrated?"

This is a multi-faceted answer. The first part has to do with your vision now. For we would ask you to examine the way that you phrase the question. Through your phraseology, you created a situation where at this present time you were not receiving what you desired. And so you were seeing that in the present time it was being withheld from you. And each time you see that, you bring forward a creation of frustration. Instead, we suggest that you see yourself as having it, that you affirm that you have it. And you say, "Well how can that be when I don't physically have it, and I humanly don't have it." We would say to you that you are working on your higher consciousness. You are working on the part of you that is sitting in the audience, not the part of you that is on the stage (from our previous theatrical example). This part of you is present on the "plane of creativity" that we described before.

From the perspective of the part of you that is sitting in the audience, you **do** have it. And as you continually call it to you, and as you continually affirm it, then you are able to draw it to you on the earth plane. From the human perspective that may seem crazy, but from the perspective of truth, you are creating it on the plane of creativity and empowering yourself to accept it on the earth plane.

Visualize your soul energy sitting in the audience of a theatre. Visualize your soul energy having everything that you need. Then see yourself walking up onto the stage and giving it to the part of you that is the actor on the stage. See yourself as the actor embracing it, and having it, and keeping it, and holding it. That is a way to use the symbology to bring and create events through the prism of your higher self. And let it then manifest on the earth plane in this dimension of your human self.

The second thing we would say to you about this is that you must continually examine why you believe you **need** something. For this portion of our talk to you, we would say that your motivations have changed to some degree as you have evolved. And so you have similar destinations, but different motivations. It is very difficult to create out of a feeling of lack. It is very difficult to create something that you desire, for you feel that it would compensate for something you believe that you lack. Because that is not creating in a creative space that is aligned with unconditional love. So then, you would see yourself on this plane of creativity **having** everything.

Question: But if I don't really **feel** that I **do** have it, then I'm pretending. I'm not **feeling** it. It's like affirming that I have everything, but I don't **feel** that.

MASTERS: Yes. What we would say to you is that in your safe space, you may pretend that you already have it. You may visualize yourself with it, feel the emotions of having it, and work with it. And what you are truly doing is creating. For when you are in your safe space in that way, you have moved a part of your consciousness onto the plane of creativity. And in that plane of creativity, you are truly creating it so that it may then be accepted on the level of the human self. You must also believe that it is possible for you to create with your beliefs.

We would use an example to illustrate how this works. This is the example of when you tell a lie ten times, it becomes a truth. So in this situation, where you are in your creative space, and you "pretend" that you have it, in this situation you are telling yourself that you have it. You are shifting your perception to reflect the fact that you already have it. And as you continually shift your perception to see that you have it, what you really and truly have done is opened yourself to receive it. For on the level of the plane of creativity it has already existed. However, it could not fit through your channel to make it into the plane of your human existence. So affirmative visualization and prayer is an integral part of the process. Focus not on the frustration that you feel. Focus not on the past where it has not occurred, for you have not been able to accommodate it through your channel. Focus only on the present where you are constantly increasing the capacity of your channel to attract and retain joy. Focus only on the bright future that you are creating for yourself with every breath, for with every breath you ingest more light. As you focus on the past, or as you focus on a specific situation of lack, you continually recreate that situation of lack. We would call our recommendation "play acting for GOD." You may call it "fake it until you make it".

Question: So when you focus on what you lack, you continue to create a situation of lack?

MASTERS: Exactly. Yes. We would also say here in this situation, again, to focus not on the lack of what you have, and to focus not on the lack within yourself. Know that you are full and complete as you are. For the light of GOD, which shines within you, makes you full and complete, for it is all that you are. For it moves past any illusion that you have about yourself, and any illusion that you have about your human limitations. Also we would say to you do not blame yourself for what you perceive as failures of your past. For they were simply objective experiences to propel you to your current state of being "at one" at all times, in all ways, with the light of GOD, which constantly feeds you.

We would also suggest that you express your frustration through your body in the appropriate time and in the appropriate place (your safe space of prayer and meditation). You can use your voice to scream or moan. You can pound on a pillow to release your frustrations. You can "talk it out" to vent your frustrations. You are learning to express through your body, and to express you anger at whatever target it needs to be expressed towards. For what you are simply doing is expressing it to the light, which takes it up and transforms it, and moves that portion of frustration and anger out from your energy. So use your body in this process and that will be very useful for you.

Question: When you say "use it in the appropriate way," would that be by ourselves, or would it be in front of the person that we are angry with, or in the situation we are angry with? You are saying use it in the proper place.

MASTERS: The broad parameters that we would offer you there would be to express in a time and a place where you would not harm yourself or others. And that could be with someone with whom you are angry, or it could be alone. If you are alone you can visualize that person sitting in front of you, and "get it off your chest" as if they are there even though they are not physically there.

Author's Comments

The process described here is the process of Emotional Release, which will be covered more fully in Chapter 7, Transforming Your Consciousness. Emotional Release is a key part of your spiritual transformation. The "Emotional Release Process" is also outlined fully in the Author's book ***"Pathways to Inner Peace": Lifesaving Processes for Healing Heart, Mind and Soul.***

Your Divine Nature

Moving Toward the Heart of GOD

It is our joy, and pleasure and honor that we work with you tonight in this way. For you have all had an initiation of sorts. You see, initiations may occur in the most mundane of activities as you open and move to a new level of enlightenment, as your energy expands to accommodate more of the light from our Creator. You have *all* had experiences this past week which have led you to open in wonderful ways. So we would begin this process, and this session, by congratulating you on the opening that you each individually realized. For in your individual opening you create more of a space for the Light that comes from the heart of GOD to dwell. So that it may manifest on the earth, and support the healing of the earth, and of all beings who inhabit the earth at this time. Therefore, your task is a divine one. So again, we would thank you for your gift of service and congratulate you.

We would also suggest that you continue shifting your view of yourself, so that you begin to see yourself more and more as we see you. You *are* beings and vessels of Light. The Light which you contain, which you are, is of infinite beauty. It is of infinite power. It is of infinite wisdom. It is of infinite strength. It is of infinite clarity. It is a treasure. It is a wonderful gift to humanity, and it is a wonderful gift to *all* worlds of existence. For your Light brings and expands the light of GOD in creation.

So it is important for you to see yourself as this treasure more, and more, and more. As you see yourself as this treasure, you will create and realize the fruits of treasuredom. You will cherish yourself, and thus others will cherish you. You will love yourself, and thus others will love you. You will revere yourself and thus others will revere you. This may seem egotistical from the level of the false-ego, however in truth this is true. For as you respect, love and revere yourself, you vibrate with that energy, which is the energy of unconditional love. As you vibrate with this energy of unconditional love, you attract more of this energy to you. Therefore you complete your task more quickly and more effortlessly on this earth plane. Your task being, once again, simply to absorb, and enjoy, and experiment, and play and create with the Light that you are, and that you draw to you. So we would congratulate you on moving to a new level and taking one more step towards the heart of GOD.

Your Expanding Consciousness

As you move more and more towards the heart of GOD, we would talk a little more about a subject that we discussed briefly before. We discussed briefly living parallel existences and having portions of your consciousness resident in several existences at once. We would begin this discussion with our old, and now comfortable, example of the bubble of expanding Light that is you. As you bring more light into your being, your bubble of Light, or your auric consciousness expands, it enables you to hold more Light. This additional light draws to it even more Light in this wonderful upward spiral. As this process continues, you are able to merge with, and contain more aspects of your soul's energy. More aspects of your soul's energy are connected to Infinite Intelligence, and more aspects of your soul's energy exists on many planes and in many realms at once. As you access more and more of this, you will find that your consciousness will be drawn and drift to different planes of existence in what you might consider daydreams. Where you suddenly come back to your human consciousness and realize that you have been immersed in another consciousness, if only for a moment. Many of these other realms in which you will find yourself being immersed, will be areas of your human consciousness which bubbles up from your subconscious mind for healing or for examination.

In the example that we extract from the Channel's consciousness, the Channel was in a business meeting, and yet found that his consciousness was fully located in 1977 driving from Sears to home and listening to an 8-track tape of the Emotions singing a song called "Rejoice". When the Channel came back to consciousness he thought, "Wow! It is like I was there!" And yes, he was. For he tapped into another level, or aspect, or the soul's infinite consciousness as it had become available as part of the sum total of his expanding auric consciousness. And so we would say this to you to tell you, and to reassure you not to be afraid. To understand that this is a natural and normal part of your expansion. Understand, once again, that your path is being guided in a very meticulous way. You are being protected and surrounded at all times in Light. A*ll* that you have to do to continue to experience our protection and our presence is to call out and invoke more and more of that Light to envelop you. For as you invoke the Light, you actually give it permission to work for you. We then have more of your permission to come closer and to touch with you.

Your Psychic Awareness

We give you this example of the expanding consciousness as a preamble to the psychic awareness, which is also a natural process of opening to Light. For as you open to the Infinite Intelligence which is connected *through* your eternal self, you realize that in an almost effortless way, that you reach this phase. You find that you have more psychic awareness without straining and without impatience. As you open more and more of your energy to the unconditional love of GOD, and Infinite Intelligence that you are a part of, that Intelligence naturally manifests through you in many ways. You remove the veil that has separated you from *our* world. So we would say also in this endeavor, be not afraid. Understand that once again your path is being guided in a very meticulous way, and know that we are with you. Now you may find this psychic opening to become more clear and more real to you, specifically with people with whom you are already involved. You initially will find that you have more insights and more connection, and a deepening link with the family members and close friends that you are already involved with initially. Eventually, and for some of you it has happened already, you will find also that you have subtle insights into the consciousness of others, even strangers, as they approach. This may help you and this may support your path of growth.

We would limit our discussion of your psychic growth and development to this simple statement of awareness. Because you see, we see things very objectively. There is much emphasis on the earth plane placed on psychic development. For psychic development is seen as a rare and cherished gift. It is a wonderful gift to be able to draw on other insights and perspectives such as ours, yes. But it is a gift that you *all* have. So we would not in any way disempower you by placing undue emphasis on the ability to draw information from other realms. **The ability to draw information from other realms is only as important as what is done with the information when it is drawn.** Is the information used to grow spiritually? Is the information used to promote what we would call the "good news" of GOD's unconditional love, and complete love for **every** being?

So the information is only as important as its usage. **You** are using the information to grow. This serves the purpose of expanding Light on the planet. So do not place undue emphasis on the bearer of the information, **do** place undue emphasis on the **use** of the information. Yes, you **all** have the ability to grow and strengthen your own channel's ability to draw information from other realms. We are working with each and every one of you to so do in a way that is comfortable for you in the time that is a part of your Divine plan. That may not necessarily coincide with your ego's plan. It does, however, coincide with the Divine plan. Prayer and meditation are useful tools for strengthening your connection. For in prayer and meditation you open yourself, and you invoke the Light of GOD more deeply within your center, practice depriving the outer senses and sharpening the inner senses.

Question: You gave the example of remembering something in the past, and the feeling like of being there. Are you referring to any kind of memories that we might have from previous times, or is it some special type of memory that is in this category?

MASTERS: Many times these memories may appear quite random. We would continue explaining this by explaining the process of dreams, and the purpose of dreams. Dreams have served many purposes. One purpose of dreams is for the brain to categorize information and stimuli in such a way that it would not clutter the brain's memory and functioning. We would use a mechanical example: When you have a computer, there are many "temporary" files that exist in the computer. And often times many, many, many temporary files are stored deeply within the inner workings of the computer until the computer is completely turned off. When, and only when, the completely turned off computer has a chance to rest and regenerate are those old temporary files destroyed to some degree, or eliminated. When the computer is left on for a very long time, and those old temporary files become voluminous, they jam the computer's memory. The computer cannot function optimally. So you see, when you sleep, a very similar thing occurs. And we would give you an example.

You may have seen a billboard, either in your active or in your passive perception, during the course of the day. We would call "passive perception" the fact that you physically saw the billboard, but you did not consciously think about it. It was in you line of sight, and it registered in your brain subconsciously, but you were not conscious of it. But this billboard triggered a thought which could not be completed because it was not a part of your consciousness. However when you go to sleep, that picture of the billboard is like an old temporary file in the computer. It must then be categorized, as if it is put in a card catalog, in its perfect place. It must be stored, or in some other way it must change form. If it does not, it will stay at what we will call the "top of your memory," and therefore impede your brain from functioning well.

You know this, for you know that when humans become sleep deprived, they begin hallucinating. For that hallucination is the brain's way of reviewing, responding to and categorizing, and filing away that old extraneous data in a **deeper** place, so that it no longer impedes the functioning of the, let us call it the "outer memory," of the brain. So when you are having an experience where you are drawn back to an event that occurred, in many cases it is a random event. There is a subtle message as this random event works with you in subtle ways. We will illustrate this by moving back to the example we gave from the channel's experience. In that example, there was a time (in 1977) when the channel was driving the car from Sears, where the channel worked, while listening to a song on the 8-track tape. The song was entitled "Rejoice." The channel, in your vernacular, "got happy" listening to that song. So when the channel's consciousness was drawn back to that time in a business meeting, a subtle (or should we say not-so-subtle) signal and reminder was sent to the channel to "rejoice!" For this was a part of the channel's expanded consciousness.

You see the consciousness of Light is always drawn to that which affirms and reflects it. So the channel's consciousness was drawn to joy. Your consciousness, as it expands, may be drawn to other experiences either in your current life, or in other experiences of your soul, either real or imagined, that would help it to grow in whatever way is necessary at any given time. This is a part of the expanded consciousness. It is continually updating itself. For you see, the computer is simply a small crude replica of the human brain, which is a small and individualized replica of the mind of GOD which holds the Infinite Intelligence.

We pause now for healing.

Psychic Development

Question: Using the analogy of the computer is very interesting because I certainly hope that my psychic growth and development is not as hard as my learning the computer. Because I've been having a really hard time and I need some help.

MASTERS: We would say that your psychic development will be quite effortless. It is not something that you have to strain for, or practice. For what would be the purpose of straining and practicing something that should be effortless and fun? The objective of meditation is simply to *know* yourself and to *know* GOD, and therefore to know that you and GOD are one. For as you know yourself, and as you know GOD, you realize that there is no separation between the two. That there is no difference between the two. One is simply an individualized expression of the whole. The part is simply a piece of the whole. In knowing this, your spiritual growth and development happens naturally and effortlessly.

You see, the human mind *always* breaks things down and categorizes them. The human mind perceives that it is finite, and perceives things in a finite way, where all must be ranked and categorized. However, in doing so, it ranks one who has developed psychically above one who has not. So there may be an inherent feeling of lack, or inadequacy, if one is not "psychic." This is an illusion. Psychic development is simply a natural outgrowth of spiritual development. Seek Ye first the Kingdom of Heaven, and all else shall follow. The Kingdom of Heaven, is the spiritual growth and development that unifies you with the heart of GOD, and connects you with the mind of GOD, and the rest will take care of itself in a wonderfully natural and organic way. Therefore, it will not seem like work. If it seems like work, then you know that it is time to play. For you are here to play.

Question: I have a question. I recognize, from past classes, that psychic development is a by-product of becoming closer to GOD. I can understand that. I guess I want to know, how do I get there faster? I've taken lots of classes, I've gone out of state to take classes, I meditate, I come to classes like this, and I'm still not hearing, I'm still not seeing. I'm still not getting intuitions. What do I do? What do I need to do? Why isn't it happening?

MASTERS: We would draw your attention to the discussion that we had with respect to creating prosperity because the concept is the same. When you send out a desire, you might ask, "What is attached to the desire?" Is there anxiety attached to the desire? Is there a motivation attached to the desire that is a motivation of lack, as opposed to a motivation of fullness? Is there a belief that through psychic development one's issues would magically dissolve? That is putting the cart before the horse. One's issues are dissolved when one chooses to dissolve them. By dissolving one's issues, the conduit to GOD is opened. For more Light can then work through the conduit, and the information that is the Light becomes more apparent to the recipient when the issues that have blocked the light are healed.

Do not judge yourself, for you are doing nothing wrong. Just understand, as you do, that you needn't turn what can be a wonderful, beautiful journey into an exhausting sprint that has no joy. Understand that the process of unfolding is happening in a way that is for your greatest good, and for the greatest good of all. Imagine if you will, the beautiful lotus that sprouts from seed, and blooms, and perishes **all in one hour.** That lotus' life expression would probably be much richer and fuller, and that lotus would probably fulfill its task, which is to experience, exhibit and share beauty and joy, more fully if its unfoldment happened gradually in a peaceful way. So that more would appreciate more fully its gifts. We would offer to you the following prayer:

Mother/Father GOD, I open to the journey to Your heart. I open to the Light which emanates from Your heart and draws me back to my home, which is within Your heart. I ask that this journey happen in an effortless way and in a way that is for my greatest good. I release all anxiety about moving back home. I release all fear about moving back home. For I know that my journey will be a wonderful one, filled with beauty and joy, and exploration, and appreciation for all that I may create on my way back home. I thank you for this opportunity fully to express, and experience, and create on my path back to you. AMEN.

Your Divine Nature

Peace be with you. You will move soon to a deeper level of peace with many of the aspects of your life. You will be able to release more and more of your anxieties. And know that where you are at any given time is perfect, and where you need to be in order to continue your journey. Each experience that you have shows you where you are on the right path to get back to home, and where you may be veering from the most direct way back home. Where you are on the right path, there would not be anxiety, or fear or frustration. There would be an effortless synchronicity. Where you are not on a path that is more synchronicitous, it would move you back into alignment with the path that is for your greatest good. When you are on a path that is not in alignment with your greatest growth, you experience manifestations of misalignment such as discomfort, inconvenience, pain and suffering. Those manifestations of misalignment would cause you to cry out, as you have done, for the guidance that would place you squarely on the path back to the heart of GOD.

Question: The anxiety and frustration I do feel. Because I feel like I would be further along than I am. But the fear, I don't feel. Are these things that are subconscious that are coming to the surface?

MASTERS: Yes and no. You see, anxiety and frustration are, to a large degree, manifestations of fear. Imagine a 2,000lb grand piano that is suspended above your head, and is held by a rope that is frayed. As you look up, you would feel anxiety. You would feel anxious to move from that space because if you did not move, you would be crushed. If your feet were embedded in cement, you would feel frustration because you would want to move, but you would feel unable to move. This too would be a manifestation of your root fear that the piano would fall and crush you. Does this illustrate the relationship?

Question: Yes. So what is my root fear of going back home?

MASTERS: Your root rear is not a fear of going back home. Your root fear is a fear of what has been manifest on your journey. You fear that you would create more pain and suffering. In the past, what has been manifest has been created out of fear in order to show you your fears. Thus, there have been anxiety-producing situations on your path back home. So what you must understand is that you are now creating with a new paradigm that is based on love, acceptance, expansion, peace, joy, and your unlimited nature. Therefore it can create only that which is a reflection of its love, peace, joy, and unlimited nature, so you no longer have to fear that on your journey you would experience pain and suffering. In summary, the root fear is not a fear of the journey home, it is a fear of what would be encountered on the journey. As you continually move your consciousness in alignment with unconditional love, and as you continually release the fears and anxieties, the energy of unconditional love becomes more and more a part of you, and becomes a larger part of the energy with which you create. You cannot create situations that would cause pain and suffering. So we would say to you that you do not have to fear. This may seem like theory to you now. So we would suggest that you continually affirm the following:

I do not have to fear. I do not have to fear. I do not have to fear. My Father is all powerful. My Father is all loving. My Father holds infinite wealth and would not withhold from me. My Father is all loving and would not punish me. My Father is all powerful and would protect me.

Imagine how you would feel in your human mind to understand who your Father truly is: the wealthiest being, the most powerful being, and the most loving being who would give to you everything and withhold from you nothing. With this, you have no reason to fear.

Question: First I want to thank you and the other beings of Light in this room for the energies that were conveyed to me last time which allowed me to release so much, and I think it was not just this life, but other lives as well that were involved. It could not have happened without that, I believe. But what's on my mind this week, is just for enough healing to get me through the waiting for my situation to evolve because it's going very slowly.

MASTERS: We would say to you that we have much empathy for you. We try, as best we can, to view situations from your perspective, where time is your prison. We continue to send you the healing, and you accept it quite wonderfully, to open yourself to the deep, deep cleansing that occurs for you now. You have answered your own question. For yes, you are counter-balancing many, many eons of misalignment. Many subtle misalignments are being healed now. You have chosen this time to incarnate and to come forward because this is a time that you knew would be your earliest opportunity to move back to the earth plane and heal yourself of these misalignments in such an intense way. Only now is there sufficient Light to enable this healing to occur. You are transforming wonderfully, and your process continues as swiftly as it can. For there must always be a balance between the swiftness in your realm of the process, and the amount of transformation that you can withstand through your human vessel at any given time. Do you understand this relationship?

We will explain. You see, you have chosen to transform many, many levels of consciousness. You have chosen to do so quite swiftly. Therefore, there is an intensity in your process of purification. Of course, we must balance the intensity with what you can withstand at any given time. You will never, and are never, and will never be given more than you can withstand. For we are guiding, and protecting, and supporting you. Yet we are giving you all that you ask for. We are continually reaching balance with you, and we will continue to do so. You are protected. Be blessed.

Question: I feel a little funny asking this, because I feel like it's been answered in many ways already. I just don't feel like I'm quite putting everything together for myself so that I really am dealing with it. I'm not quite sure how to say it. I have a great deal of trouble meditating and focusing. I'm sure that I need a lot of emotional release there on several different issues. But I guess what I'm asking for is a little clarification of what I think it's related to, which is the conscious memory of being taken into the light and experiencing that love, then coming back here, losing that, turning away from it. I started feeling a really intense homesickness. I think I just came a little too close.

MASTERS: We would share with you a new way to view your situation. You may travel home, which is the dominant belief that many have on many level....that belief that you must leave your physical body and travel home to the Kingdom of Heaven, resident within the heart of GOD. The good news, as Light becomes more prevalent here on earth, is that you may bring your **home** to **you**. You can experience not only the joys and freedoms of being in spirit, but you may do so while being physically manifest on the earth plane, which adds yet another wonderful, tangible, physical, focused dimension to your ability to express through your soul.

So your belief that you must "travel" to get home, and that your home is unavailable to you now, is a belief from the past that no longer applies. For there is enough Light on earth now that enables you to **be home** wherever you are. Imagine yourself in a car that formerly had needed to travel to a destination and be lodged in a garage. Now imagine yourself transforming yourself from a car, that must travel home to a garage, to a camper that carries all the amenities of home with it, yet it has the mobility to explore. You have that ability. You have the ability to experience the amenities of home while having the mobility to explore and navigate this wonderful, beautiful, experience-filled rich earth plane.

Of course, based on your perceptions of the past, you may not see it as such. It does have its challenges that are experienced in human form. But we would say that yours is a gift. For most humans believe that they must travel home. You now know that you have a camper that travels with you and brings you all the amenities of home. In order to experience what we discuss more fully, you might use that visual image. See yourself going into your camper, or any other sacred space that has all the amenities of home. We specifically suggest for you a camper because it connotes something tangible and earth bound, yet it connotes something that offers comfort, convenience, respite, shelter and peace. So we would suggest that you visualize creating this wonderful camper for yourself that has all the amenities, comforts, and peace and protection that you desire. Imagine yourself going into this space and being comfortable there. Imagine seeing what wonderful gifts and amenities it has for you. By doing this visualization you will enhance your ability to concentrate.

Question: I have a question that I hope I can formulate. First of all, I'm so excited about being Christ-ed. It has exciting possibilities for me. Actually, I already know. It is just so wonderful to be affirmed about being a Light bearer. So I am glad about that. I thought about that when we were asked to reflect about that. There were a few fears that came up for me, too. But I'm wondering, as I'm being Christ-ed, what does that mean in the context of my day-to-day, the little things. I mean the illusions that are going on. Will it be to a point where this won't bother me? That the little petty stuff going around at work, or the bill that hasn't been paid, do you know what I mean?

MASTERS: We do understand. What will happen with you day-to-day concerns with the seemingly insignificant and petty aspects of your life that now cause, in their most innocuous form, irritation, and in their most seemingly sinister form, pain and suffering? You see, being Christ-ed means having so much of the Light of GOD living within your energy field, and vibrating within your energy field, that it consumes and subsumes all else. Being Christ-ed means having such a direct, and strong, and deep connection with the heart of GOD that you **are** GOD, in a sense. You are the true individual expression of the infinity and expansiveness of GOD while in human form.

As this process occurs, you see the illusion for what it is. It no longer has power over you. For you know that it is not in truth. You also know in a very deep way that you are protected. For as you vibrate only in Light, you only create that which is only in Light. Nothing that is of the illusion can touch you, or harm you. Nor will it irritate you. For those irritants are due to fears, misperceptions and judgments. Your fears, your misperceptions and your judgments will fall away quite naturally. WE are working with each of you in a way that would enable this to happen with a minimal amount of disruption. Do not fear that you will lose your families, your friends, your loved ones, or any trappings that you have an affinity to. For you will have all your heart's desires. You will have them, however, with joy, and peace.

Question: I don't have a question, because all of my questions have been answered as I've been soaking up all of this Light, and writing, getting answers. And they've been wonderful answers. But I just wanted to make contact and tell Spirit that it's exciting that this technique has worked and about all of the progress I feel that I've made over the last 10 weeks.

MASTERS: We share your excitement, and we share your gratitude, and we thank **you** for opening to the process of your enlightenment more deeply. We thank you and we bless you all. Words cannot express, so we hope that this final embrace will express our love for you. Please prepare for this final energy embrace.

CHAPTER 5.
THE HEALING POWER OF THE UNIVERSE

It is with love, and joy, and humility that we offer our light to you now in this way. You have all absorbed much light. You all have grown significantly during the course of this week. You all have used the light that has been made available to you to align your energy centers, to cleanse and purify your energy fields, and to expand your energy bodies so that you could accommodate even more light. This circle of light is the spiral of healing. And we will discuss this in more detail now.

We will begin the discussion of healing with the simple phrase "as above, so below." Many of you have heard this phrase many times. As above, so below. In your minds, you think of this as a part of the prayer that you utter "on earth as it is in Heaven." They are similar phrases with the same intent. The intent of these phrases is to communicate a truth to you. That truth is that all is created in the realm of expanded vibration first. This realm is the realm of reality where consciousness and energy is expanded (for your earth plane is the illusion). This is the realm that that you normally do not have much access to as a human. However, **in this realm all is created.** Then it manifests on the earth plane. As above, so below.

The energy patterns appear, and coagulate, and form on our plane of existence. Then they coagulate and form on the earth plane as a reflection of the energy in our realm, which is the realm of creativity. So you see, the energies of misalignment, which may cause illness or "dis-ease" are evident in our realm much, much sooner than when they manifest on the earth plane in your physical bodies, or in situations. By the same token, your energies of alignment occur on our plane of existence and then manifest on the earth plane in wellness and in wholeness. The most important part of this process for you is your awareness.

Awareness is a term that we would use expansively. For in this case, awareness means not only your thoughts and your beliefs, but also your perceptions and the experiences that are a part of your emotional and energy body that you are conscious of, and those that you are unconscious of. All of these factors make up your awareness. When all of these factors are aligned with unconditional love, your beliefs are based on unconditional love, then the portion of the energy that is about you that is your auric consciousness, is aligned with unconditional love. Then the energy centers in the physical body are aligned with unconditional love, and the light flows through in an obstructed, unblocked way.

You may ask then, "How can one's experiences from the past be of unconditional love when many of those experiences have not seemed to be loving?" Even those experiences of the past, in the larger realm of your soul's infinite existence, have been designed to move you into alignment. For they have been designed to trigger you into emotional release by showing you where your energy was not aligned with unconditional love.

When past experiences are seen in this light (through the prism of the infinity of your soul) then they too can be loved unconditionally, for they have been the perfect tools for you to move into love. So with that, even those experiences from the past which make up your auric consciousness which can be healed and transformed through the emotional release that we discuss can be perfect. They are used in their perfect way for healing, and thus can be of unconditional love.

So we would say that healing begins on our plane with your request, your constant request, or as the soul's request for healing. Healing then manifests with experiences that show you where the healing is needed. Those experiences, when used for their greatest good, show you where there are loving energies and where there are not. Through prayer, release and meditation, those unloving, unmoving, disharmonious energies are made harmonious. And the healing occurs.

We would now point to one barrier to healing that can be quite pervasive which is what we call the "false-ego." The false-ego is the part of the human being that identifies most strongly with the earth plane, and the trappings of the earth plane. The false-ego places utmost and paramount importance on the earth plane and these trappings. The false-ego does not realize yet that these trappings are simply tools, and toys and props in the never-ending drama of the soul to come back to alignment with GOD.

The false-ego fears its annihilation. The false-ego feels that through the transformation and the merging of the soul's energy with the human energy, that it would be destroyed. It does not simply understand that it is being transformed in a loving and gentle way through this process. The false-ego is the part of the self that feels separate from the soul, unloved by GOD and guilty. The false-ego is the personality. It is the part of the being that feels that it would never be enough. It is never quite satisfied. It feels that there is always something more, and it is always found wanting. The false-ego is what you would call the name, rank and serial number of the human being. The false-ego is the part of the human being that is attached to the earth plane.

Now we would say all these things in description of the false-ego, not to judge it, but to help you to understand its perspective. For the perspective of the false-ego is limited. It does not see the infinity of life. It does not see the abundance of GOD. Therefore, it fears that it would not have enough. It does not see GOD's unconditional love, and so fears that it will be punished for the guilt that it feels, because it perceives that it is separate.

The false-ego fears this punishment and annihilation to the point that it would do anything to survive. It would manipulate. It would control. It would hurt or harm others. It would denigrate others to make itself feel superior, when in fact it was feeling inferior and needed to compensate for those feelings of inferiority. It would feel fear. It would act out on this fear in anger, and rage, and hatred towards others, or towards facets of itself.

Again, we would say do not judge the false-ego. By understanding the origin of the false-ego, and its original divine intent, you can release your judgments of it so that you may use it more effectively to support your healing process. The original purpose of the false-ego was to make humans aware of their physical dimension during the earlier stages of "the descent into matter". At the earliest stages of your evolution on earth, you were uncomfortable in a physical body because you knew of yourself essentially as spiritual beings. You had difficulty navigating the earth plane, and needed a "compass" to anchor you to the physical plane. The "compass" was the false-ego, which made you constantly aware of your physical nature.

However, as you continued to evolve, you became less and less aware of your spiritual nature, and more and more aware of your physical nature. There was an imbalance, and the imbalance in your energies, which ties your energies into knots of anger, frustration and confusion is now what creates the pain and suffering that triggers you to move back into balance. Yes, the false-ego is behind this, but it actually thinks that it is still protecting you, by helping you to navigate the earth plane. When you see the false-ego in this way, you see that it is actually acting out of love -- a love that is misguided. Therefore, the false-ego has served a wonderful, divine purpose and should not be judged. It should simply be used as a tool to move you toward healing.

You might consider it to be a child that is hungry. An infant that is hungry cries to get the attention that it needs. It then must be supported, loved and nurtured. By the same token, love and nurture your false-ego out of its pain. Love and nurture yourself out of the energy blockages that show up in your life as pain, suffering and disease.

The false-ego is what is tying these energies into the knot that keeps the energies dense and contracted, and keeps the energies from drawing through light in a perfectly aligned way to support expansion, and growth and alignment. So the false-ego is what is being transformed through the process of expanded awareness, prayer and meditation. This process helps you to align more and more with the energy of the eternal soul, and less and less with the energy of the false-ego.

Emotional release enables you to untie the knots caused by the continual contraction of energy, and this facilitates healing. This facilitates healing for yourself because you are more in alignment with unconditional love. It facilitates healing for other because as you become more and more aligned with unconditional love, you then transmit subtle energies to others which helps to unblock them and begin the process of healing their energy as well. So when you feel contraction, fear, rage, anger, pain, sadness, grief, or any other emotion that would cause you to close off your light from the source that feeds it constantly, understand that it is the false-ego.

Accept those feelings. Accept that they are there to teach you where the false-ego exists so that you may transform it and identify more and more with the soul, and less and less with the name, rank and serial number on the earth plane. This is a process which becomes easier and easier with practice.

Awareness of the ego is the first step. Awareness of the source of the ego's pain, or confusion, or misperception is the second step. Awareness of the misperception itself is the third step. Releasing the awareness of the misperception so that you may have an awareness of the truth in its place, the substitution once again of unconditional love for that which unloving is the next step. This is healing.

In summary, healing is the alignment of your awareness or consciousness with unconditional love. It begins on the plane of creativity, or shall we way in the world of reality where we dwell, and it then is manifested on the earth plane where your human consciousness, which is but a speck in the infinity of your soul, exists. As your awareness is drawn into alignment, and every aspect of your awareness is brought into alignment with unconditional love, your human component is healed physically, mentally and the circumstances of your human existence are also healed. As you open to more and more of our light, this process continues.

One last thing that we would say to you about this process is that at times it may feel as if things for you are getting worse, instead of better. It may feel that after a deep, deep healing you may have drawn to you even more discord. In fact, after a deep healing, you have drawn to you more power to heal. With that power to heal, you are then able, and strong enough, to delve more deeply into your awareness and heal even more aspects of this awareness. So you are then given additional aspects of your awareness to heal, and they are shown to you through the situations and circumstances that may appear to momentarily get worse instead of better. You must remember that you are never given more than you are capable of healing. And we are always there to help and support you. And as your awareness expands, you understand this also.

Question: The discord and disharmony experienced by the false-ego one day this week were very, very hard to deal with. It took a whole day of grappling with it to come to the surrender, and the healing, and the realignment asked for. I felt as if the next morning a "spiritual" muscle had been flexed and strengthened. I also felt that this had to be done in such a drastic manner so that I would know that I was moving toward alignment.

MASTERS: You are absolutely correct in your perception. You see, true awareness comes through experience. The experience that you had gave you a very strong, a very visceral, and a very deep experience of the process of which we speak. It gave you the strength to continue with this process, and the faith that this process is for your greatest good and is in truth. For prior to this experience, on many levels, this truth was simply an esoteric theory for you. But now you truly realize its deep truth and the power and strength that it has to heal you on every level. You are now in a better position to use this wonderful tool more frequently. However we would say to you that not all situations will cause such, shall we say, violent reactions. You see, the process becomes easier and easier, just like when you lift heavy weights. The more you lift them, the easier they are to lift. We would confirm also that you were not alone in this experience. There are those of us who are emissaries of the Light that is emitted from the heart of GOD whose task it is to heal and transform you, who gently and lovingly guided you through this process and will continue to guide you for as long as necessary. Know too that you have created a deep opening for more of your soul energy to infiltrate your human consciousness and to guide you more effortlessly in the path of joy, and peace and abundance. This too will be the results of your efforts. Be blessed and in the light, and know that you are always held in our light, in our love.

Question: Regarding this process of emotional healing, it feels like it works best for me in the company of at least one other person. However when I have tried to do this in the past, I have run into a difficulty in communicating what I wanted. And I am not sure whether to pursue this again with another community, or to try to do more alone.

MASTERS: The process of emotional healing, and the steps that must be taken in this process, are not well understood by many. As with most endeavors, there is no right way and there is no wrong way. There is only the intent. The intent is always aligned with the greatest good and the highest purpose. So however you choose to follow the path of emotional release is your choice, and a function of your desire. In the situations that you describe, the energy that infiltrated the situations was one of fear. You see, there is fear of this process on two levels. There is the fear felt by the false-ego that it would be destroyed through this process. Part of the false-ego does not understand that it is simply being transformed, and not destroyed. There is also the fear that the human consciousness has of the emotional body. For the human consciousness is very aware of the destructive capabilities of the emotional body, and does not truly understand in full the productive capabilities of the emotional body. This fear manifested in these instances as difficulty, or discomfort, with the process. Know that even if you choose to do, or pursue, the process alone, you are not alone. For we are with you. You are adept at perceiving our energies. You may use this facility as an integral part of your process so that you know that you are never alone with this. You have been guided here for this purpose.

We would also address a fear that the human consciousness has of what we will call the "gapped rage." The gapped rage is a term that is used to describe an energy that must be moved out of the energy field, that has been unmoving for eons and eons of time, and exists at the very deep level in the consciousness of the individual. This energy has the capability to manifest as destructive, if a safe and comfortable environment is not established, and if a process of light and protection is not invoked when the process of emotional release is pursued. Now to a large degree, simply by pursuing the process of emotional release, there is an invocation of the light of protection. However, the awareness of this gapped rage and its potential for destruction also causes subconscious fear of the process of emotional release. That is why we say that establishing a safe environment where you cannot harm yourself or others is ideal in practicing emotional release. When experiencing the gapped rage, you feel as if the earth within you is moving. And it is. You feel almost as if a portion of you has moved out of you, and it has. This channel has experienced that deep level of release. Many of you will experience that deep level of release. When proper preparation is made, and proper guidance is invoked, it will happen in an effortless and loving way. For you see, many times what is being released is simply triggered by the current circumstances, but is truly a release of things that have been held within the emotional body for eons of time.

Question: When I view myself in light of what you were saying about transforming to your higher self, as critical as I am about myself, it is difficult for me to analyze what needs to be worked on.

MASTERS: Yes. We would say that what needs to worked on is what is given to you through your experiences at any time. It is, of course, very easy to take a comprehensive inventory of yourself and come up with an endless array of items to be addressed. However, as part of the process of surrender, you may choose to surrender to the Divine plan, which would select the items from your inventory in a way that is perfect for you. The list of items in your inventory is not very long at all. They are actually quite simple, but they just repeat, and repeat, and repeat in different ways. So when you surrender to the divine plan, what you experience will trigger a reaction from you. Your task is to examine that reaction, have that reaction, become aware of that reaction, work with what is triggered, let that align you with the Light in the process that we have described before, and then move forward for you have had a healing. So you do not have to actively take your inventory. Your experiences, or shall we say the Divine plan for your life, which helps you from a level of your higher self to determine your experiences, helps you move through the inventory quite effortlessly for your experiences are a teacher. The part of one's self that is hypercritical is, of course the false-ego, which always sees that it is not enough, that it is not good enough, that it is found wanting. We would reiterate to you that you are perfect in all ways, and at all times you are perfect. For even those parts of you that feel you are "unaligned with Light" or imperfect, are perfect because they will certainly give you what you need to align with the light.

Author's Note

Throughout this book, there have been many references to emotional release. The concept of emotional release is described most fully in my book entitled ***"Pathways to Inner Peace: Lifesaving Processes for Healing Mind, Body and Soul".***

CHAPTER 6.
THE LAW OF SELF-RESPONSIBILITY

Question: My daughter is suffering from depression, and one of the manifestations of that, as well as the fact that she's 16, is that she's being very rebellious. She thinks she is very grown up all of a sudden. She wants to go out on her own and do things, and to me, that to me feels dangerous. This is where the fear comes in. I don't always know how to deal with it. I feel that there should be something else I can do to help her and I'm not quite sure what.

MASTERS: We would ask that every expression of GOD's consciousness that is present here tonight send light to this being. We would discuss for all, again, the concept of self-responsibility. And we would also discuss the concept of invoking the light of GOD in every situation. We would also discuss unconditional love. For these are the three ingredients that support the process that is being described and experienced.

The first thing that we would discuss here is self-responsibility. If a gardener places topsoil on the ground, and plants a seed, and fertilizes the plant, and waters the seed, and ensures that it receives the sun, at some point it must be the seed's choice to bloom. The gardener has done everything in her power to provide the environment that would enable the plant to bloom. However it is then the plant's choice to bloom or not to bloom. The gardener may feel in some way that her gardening skills are found wanting because the plant chooses not to bloom. But the gardener must ultimately know, and understand, that the gardener has done everything in her power. Therefore, the gardener need not feel guilty, and therefore the gardener need not fear retribution. For the gardener has not been a bad gardener. The gardener has been an excellent gardener. The choice has been the plant's. The plant alone, at that point, is responsible for its blooming. The gardener can only till the soil, lay the topsoil, sow the seed, fertilize the seed, water the plant.

The gardener can continually invoke the Grace of GOD in the process through prayer and meditation. Through working on herself to channel more light through, and by sending that light to the plant, the gardener brings herself into alignment with GOD. And therefore can transmit more light to the plant, and help the plant to transform if the plant chooses. And so the gardener opens that aspect of her life to GOD.

Question: We've talked in several sessions about unconditional love. And maybe I haven't gotten it yet. But unconditional love is not the same as unconditional acceptance of a person's behavior. Is that correct?

MASTERS: Yes. That is correct.

Question: So that you may still love someone unconditionally, and yet disapprove of their behavior, or their actions, or the way they treat other people, or the things that they do to themselves?

MASTERS: The word that is of concern in your statement is "disapprove."

Question: Because that's judgmental.

MASTERS: That is a portion of the reason that word is of concern. We talk often about unconditional love. We also talk often about self-responsibility. And the two are intertwined in a very interesting way. Self-responsibility is a form of unconditional love. For when you are able to love someone unconditionally, you are able to free them and you free yourself. You are able to free yourself from feeling any responsibility for that individual. And you are able to free that individual to learn their lessons in the way that is for their greatest good.

This often times seems theoretical. You would not enable someone to destroy themselves because the human response is always to help. The human response is always to intervene. The human response is always to give. So the concept of Divine Wisdom (also known as Spiritual Common Sense) enters into the equation. Use the Divine Wisdom that you tap into through prayer and meditation to know when you have done all that you can to help a person. Use it to know when you have done all that you must do in being responsible only for yourself, and when you can or must do that which would support your brother, or sister, on the earth plane. Use Divine Wisdom to discern.

Also use Divine Wisdom to ascertain your motivation. Are you concerned about the other individual because, if they take some course of action, they will be, in some way, unable to fulfill your needs? Are you concerned about another individual because if they take a course of action, it would be, in some way, perceived to be a bad reflection on you? These are the types of questions that you may also ask yourself. And that you may also use your Divine Wisdom to discern.

For you see, when you allow yourself to be drawn into the drama of someone else's choosing, you are not being true to your soul's path. You are letting someone else drag you into their lake of quicksand. And that may not be completely and unconditionally loving of yourself, which is where unconditional love begins. So we would say that unconditional love and self-responsibility are intertwined in a unique way. Use your divine wisdom to enable yourself to be responsible only for yourself, and not to deny or denigrate yourself by dispersing your energy in a path that has little to do with you, and most to do with another. For in doing so, you deny yourself the fruits of your growth.

We also would say when you judge another, you are also limiting your light. For that other is a reflection of the part of your consciousness, and you are judging it. And we would say instead of judging it, try as best you can to see it objectively. Seeing it objectively, understand that part of consciousness which you are judging, and therefore unable to accept, is simply a tool to show you where you have opportunity to align more with the truth of GOD's unconditional love.

What we have shared with you is quite complex. It must be understood not only intellectually, but must be understood at the deepest levels of your consciousness. What you are trying to do is shed an overlay within your consciousness that says that "I must be responsible for someone else in order to achieve my own potential, and prove my worth". We would say that this is an illusion. And through your frustration, you understand the illusion. You are learning the lesson of self-responsibility in a deep way.

We would also say that there is anger in the frustration that you feel. This anger stems from a subconscious fear that you are not fulfilling your task and will be punished as a result. A part of your consciousness believes that you were brought here this time, and in this way, to be responsible for someone else. This is karmic patterning. For you agreed, prior to this incarnation to help others "as best you can". In this situation, as best you can has already been accomplished. This is difficult. We do not deny its difficulty. So we would say to you that what we have said to others. You may always choose to send light, to draw light to you, to absorb light, and to send it to whomever you feel needs it. The other individual may choose to accept the light, or not, at that time. If the light is not accepted by the individual, then the light maybe accepted at some point in the future when the individual is open to that light. Or that light is added to the reserve of light that exists on the planet, and is available for the healing of consciousness, and life and matter on the planet. And it **is** all good. It is **all** good. It is all **good**. We send you our blessings. We send you our peace. If you could only see yourself as we see you. If you could only take off the ‘yoke" that this illusion has placed on your shoulders. If you could only see yourself as being free. And know, in truth, that you are. Be blessed.

Do not feel in any way wanting, or do not feel badly about where you are in your process. Do not feel in anyway that you have failed an assignment. For you are doing wonderful in learning very trying and difficult lessons that will ultimately free you. Do not think of what you **should be**, what you **should** say, how you **should** react. For that does not matter. What matters is that you **are**. And however you choose to be or react is fine for that time, because it is for your greatest good. So if you feel that there is something that you must release now, understand that you are safe. Understand that you are comforted. Understand that you are loved, not only by our light, but by the light contained in the others who are here with you.

Question: On the subject of unconditional love. Some time back, it felt like I was experiencing both unconditional love and anger, and frustration towards the same person. Is that really a possibility to be simultaneous?

MASTERS: It is reality. For you see, you are in the process of merging your soul energy with you human energy. And there is a wonderful mixture of the two that you exude. And what better illustration of this than feeling unconditional love, anger, and frustration simultaneously?

Question: On the same topic. While we're off being free what happens to the other person. Do you surround that person with love, and light and support? 'Cause the only thing we really need to know is that the person is safe and well taken care of, and then we feel we'll be free to go off and be happy?

MASTERS: We would say that any and every individual is always surrounded with love, light, protection and support. For you see, your human consciousness is like a cocoon. And as you open to more light, you are able to contain more and light within the cocoon. And this strengthens the being inside, which is your soul. Just as there is always light surrounding a cocoon, even when the light cannot break through the cocoon, there is always light surrounding any individual. The challenge that every individual expression of GOD's Light has is opening to the light. The task is to merge the light that you perceive **outside** of its shell, with that light with the light that lives within the shell. You do this by eliminating the shell, which is the perceptional barrier between your individual world and the collective world of light from which we speak.

Question: Yesterday my husband was diagnosed with cancer. I have a great deal of fear around this. I know this is his issue, so how do I know which part of this drama is "my stuff". How can I deal with my part of this? I'm not sure what my question is…

MASTERS: Your question is "where to draw the line". This is so important to you, and so instructional because it illustrates loving self-acceptance and the importance of continually re-filling your pitcher of light so that you may constantly pour out the light of GOD. The lesson is for the other individual, yet in truth it is also for you. Since you are here, we will relate how this impacts you. It is an opportunity to submit your deepest fears to the light of GOD for healing and transformation. This situation is an opportunity for you to get deeply in touch with your emotional body, your needs, your desires, your fears, and your issues from the past so that you may transform them and then have what you have desired for a very long time. What you have desired for a long time is a stronger, more tangible connection with the light of GOD, and a healing of your emotional body. Your emotional body is triggered into healing through this situation, and it gives you a chance to make a deeper connection with GOD by eliminating the energies that have blocked this connection. This situation "pushes the buttons" of your fears, it forces you to articulate the things that you want, and it forces you cry out to GOD in many ways, which deepens your relationship with GOD. This all propels you on a strong path of growth where you re-unite with your souls energy and you grow spectacularly over the next several months.

As this situation relates to the other individual, your task is to be kind and supportive. Your task is to use your place of peace and clarity to help this individual, because this situation will force you to continually go within to find peace and clarity. You will continually deal with your fear, your doubts about GOD's love, your anger and your rage. These feelings will force you to continually go to the "well of light" to get the healing that would quell the fires of your emotions. As you do this, you then can provide light, healing, support, information and guidance and a strong, light-filled presence to your partner. As you do this, your partner will feel the light that you pour from your "pitcher of light", and will respond optimally in his process of transformation.

Where you draw the line is as follows: You do what you can on the earth plane for your partner. You try to continually fill your "pitcher of light" by continually opening to the light of healing and transformation through your channel. This enables you to give from a position of "overflow" and keeps you from being drained and depleted. This action increases your ability to draw more light to you, and it helps both you and your partner.

There are times when you may feel depleted or overwhelmed. Give yourself permission to do so, knowing that as you do, you help not only yourself, but you also help your partner because you replenish your pitcher so you may pour again. We thank you for offering this specific illustration of how self-love is not selfish. As you increase your love for your self, you expand your ability to give love to others.

Question: I have a family member with AIDS, and my other family members who know I do healing work. My sense is that he doesn't want to be physically healed, but he wants to move towards an emotional healing. I would like any insights as to what I should do if anything.

MASTERS: First of all, we will verify that emotional healing brings about physical healing, because the emotional body creates its reflection in the physical body. Therefore, you know that in order to heal the physical body, the emotional body must be healed.

This individual has chosen a path that ultimately leads to self-love and self-acceptance (which is in essence emotional healing). This path has been chosen, even though at times on this earth plane it may seem that this individual does not want to heal. In truth, even in death there is a healing, for a healing is simply a shift in the energy patterns, thought pattern, and their manifestations so that these energies, thoughts and manifestations are back in alignment with unconditional love. So when an individual transitions back into spirit, the individual is moving back into alignment with unconditional love because the individual is moving back home, to the heart of GOD.

What you may do is to provide healing energy from a distance and if this individual chooses to accept it, he will do so and use it in a way that is for his highest good. If he is not ready to accept it, or if he accepts it and uses it to provide comfort or to facilitate his transformation, it is for his greatest good to do so. If he does not choose to use it at all, it will simply be added to the repository of light that is available for the planet and to all who are on the planet. No matter what, this healing energy will be used, and as you send out this healing energy it actually helps you to receive more energy and light, and this places you on an upward spiral. We would also advise you to try not to absorb any judgments about this situation. Try to avoid judgments such as "death is bad and undesirable" or "life is good and desirable." Both are simply different parts of the realm of infinite existence, and the soul will get whatever it needs regardless of which side of the veil it exists.

Question: How can I help a new friend along the path to healing that he so desperately needs?

MASTERS: You can help your friend by helping yourself. You already are. Any relationship, including relationships of friends who become special, are relationships that are created so that you see aspects of consciousness which are needing to be healed within you because those aspects of consciousness are reflected in the other person. So you ask yourself, "What aspect of consciousness is this person exhibiting, and what am I learning from it?" It is very easy to see another person objectively because the other person is in front of you and it is very easy to take their inventory. What you must understand is that you are giving yourself an opportunity to take your own inventory in a non-threatening way through this process. Then you work on yourself, and you heal those aspects of consciousness that are being reflected to you, understanding that they may not be at the surface level of **your** consciousness. They may be deep within your consciousness from other experiences from other existences, or you may block them out, but they are there. If they were not there, they would not be reflected to you. So you work on yourself. As you work on yourself, you continually bring more light into yourself, and that light is then moving out of you and touches the other person as well. This starts that person on their process of healing. It is very admirable and very loving to enter on a quest to "save" another. However the most effective way to "save" another is to save one's self. And in doing so, you draw the power, the energy, and the transformative capabilities to you, through you, and it helps others by default.

Imagine your quest to save another as giving unsolicited advice. As you know, unsolicited advice is rarely received in the manner in which it was given. So all you can do, and all that a relationship is to show you, is where you may heal your own consciousness. And the rest will take care of itself. For as you heal your own consciousness, and as you send this person healing light, you are actually adding to the reservoir of light that appears on the planet. And when this individual chooses to draw on that, the individual may. But of course, it must be the individual's choice due to their free will. And we thank you.

Question: I have a desire. Would you help my brother take in more light so that he can make that decision from a soul level, and so that the big changes and the permanent changes will take place? And for me, to take in more light, and to go deeper, and expand my soul energy.

MASTERS: We certainly can, are, and will continue working with you to expand your soul energy so that you may contain more light, for you have requested this many times and on many different levels. We **also** will add, and direct, and focus light onto your brother, so that if he chooses to use this light he will, in his own time and in his way. And if he chooses not to use this light in his own time and in his own way, this light would simply be added to the reservoir of light that exists on earth for overall healing. You see, each individual has the free will to create as many experiences in this realm as they need. And we cannot interrupt that free will. We can only make alternatives available and then it is the entity's choice to choose. We would send you a healing now that has to do with your comfort and peace with this situation. We of course offer compassion as we move light through to you, and we, with love, focus on what this lesson teaches you. For this lesson for you is a gift of self-responsibility. You understand, through understanding each individual's free will and use of it, their responsibility for themselves, and your responsibility for your growth. You grow for many reasons. One reason is so that you may expand the light that you are able to send to others. One reason is to increase the peace which resides within you. When you move to a deeper level of understanding of self-responsibility, you understand that when you assume responsibility for another individual, you relinquish part of your right and your desire for inner peace. For your desire for inner peace then becomes contingent on choices that another being makes. And you no longer have that power, for that other being always maintains free will. So you expand your light so that you may make more light available to others, but you relinquish responsibility for others. For that would not give you the ultimate peace that you desire, and through that peace, the ultimate ability to continue expanding your light.

Question: Yes. If that is the case, then why do we send healing to people if it is their free will. If it's their free will to accept or reject it, then is it not their free will to just take it themselves?

MASTERS: The fact that you send light to people serves several purposes. First of all, the soul's impetus is to send light. It is an automatic response of the soul. For the soul only wants to receive light, absorb it, disseminate it. That is the purpose of the soul, as repository, as a distributor. You see, the soul, the individualized soul, was developed to expand light. And therefore, that is what it does naturally. And the soul, when linked with the portion of the soul that manifests as a human consciousness, the human minds say "part of my task is to help and to send light, and therefore I will." And so it happens. But also, it also helps you. We have referred to this before as "spiritual aerobics (sending light to others, which increases your capacity for light). As you **practice** this process of ingesting, absorbing, and disseminating light, you grow your soul. You **grow** your light. You fulfill your soul's purpose. And that is why it happens.

CHAPTER 7. TRANSFORMING YOUR CONSCIOUSNESS

Question: Sometimes when I'm trying to choose between being kind and loving, and the thought comes up about being real, which means expressing other emotions. And it kind of feels like contact on a different level, or deeper level. There's a struggle involved and it feels like there's a thought that being kind and being loving is not being real. And I was wondering if spirit has any insight into where that comes from.

MASTERS: You have shown a great deal of interest in the process of emotional release and emotional healing. The reason for your interest in this is that you are being urged by your soul to open to an extremely great velocity of light; that this light is touching and wanting to transform, and this process is strengthened and facilitated through the process of emotional release. You have heard this, and you know this, and you are struggling to understand this at a deeper level. So we will offer you more insights into this process.

The misperception you carry is the perception that there is a dichotomy between being kind, and loving and good, and expressing the baser emotions which you perceive are not of light. The truth is that these "baser" emotions are light as well. For all energy is light. If you recall, the picture or image that we gave you of continuous energy, it is all light. That portion of light that is considered the "baser" part of your consciousness has not evolved to the point where it is vibrating in the way that other portions of your consciousness are vibrating. The other portions of your consciousness are trying to bring the "baser" portion along. Your higher consciousness does this by flooding your lower consciousness with light so that it can expand its vibration. However, in order for this to occur, the old non-moving energies must be released through emotional release: the cathartic wail, the expressions of anger, the release of fear, etc. This process cleanses you and gives you a greater awareness of the reason for anger, and then the light can heal the misconceptions and move that portion of your consciousness in accordance with the light; to raise it's vibration, in other words. So this process is in love. Those emotions are in love. They are seeking to evolve. They are an absence of love seeking to evolve into an awareness of love. The conflict that you face is that you believe they are not of love. We would reassure that they are. And we would reassure you that the process of having those emotions, honoring them, and honoring yourself for having them is a loving process. This process transforms you into a being that is pure light, for the areas within your energy field that are vibrating with a darker, denser energy are transformed. That transformation is one of the most loving gifts you can give to yourself or others. Do not judge yourself for having these emotions. You sometimes judge yourself for having them because you would feel that they are not worthy emotions. Remember, all is worthy because all is continuous energy. All energy has emanated from the source and is part of the source. So do not judge these feelings. Do not judge yourself for having them. Do not judge the process of transforming them from the dark, conflicted, contracting thought and energy patterns that cause and create situations that would trigger anger, rage, pain, sadness, and grief. You must understand that as you recognize the mis-perception that causes this, you become aware of the lack of love. And when you become aware of the lack of love, you can then give that part of your consciousness the love that it yearns for and evolve it into part of GOD's unconditional love. We will be working with you in a deep way on this process of emotional release as we explain the process more fully.

1) **Have the emotion.** Do not suppress it. For suppressing it only forces it back into your energy field, when the situation that has triggered the emotional release has been divinely inspired and sanctioned to help you become aware of where you are, loving

yourself completely and unconditionally, and where you are not. So have the emotion.

2) **Honor the emotion.** It is not bad. It simply is. Do not judge it. Honor it as an opportunity to evolve yourself.

3) **Honor yourself.** Do not judge yourself for having the emotion.

4) **Release the emotion.** You may use many mechanisms for this process of emotional release. You may scream, you may rant, you may rail, you may cry, you may curse, you may kick, you may punch a pillow. You hopefully are all creating safe spaces for yourself in prayer and meditation where you cannot harm yourself or others. And in this space, you can release the emotion. You may also choose other forms of emotional release. You may release through your vocal chords. You may even begin with an "aum," and feel the emotion rising out of your vocal chords and continue to emit the sound of "aum" for other sounds as the emotions move out of you. You may also choose other physical ways to release the emotion. You may choose physical exercise. You may choose a punching bag, or again, most expediently, you may choose a punching pillow.

So you have the emotion, you honor the emotion, you honor yourself, you release the emotion. After emotional release, there is a catharsis. There is a peace. What you have done is you have moved out old, unmoving energy and there is a space for more light within your energy field. And in this space comes information...an awareness.

5.) **Ask.** You may now ask to become aware of the belief that you had that caused the negative emotion. That the belief you had that caused the situation, which then triggered the seemingly negative emotion. You become aware that this belief is an error.

6.) **Pray.** You may now pray that your mind be healed and that you have a shift in your perception so that you no longer have this erroneous belief. The belief that somehow there is a portion of you that is unlovable, and therefore not vibrating in GOD's unconditional love. You have believed that this part of you deserves punishment, or pain, or suffering, or deprivation, or needs to experience fear. After asking for the awareness, you ask that your mind be healed of this misperception. This is praying for a miracle. You ask, and then you receive. Does that sound familiar? Ask and you shall receive the answer, the reason for the misperception. Then you pray that the misperception be healed. You pray that the light that enters you energy field works with your consciousness, and works with every cell of your being to retool your thought processes so that you no longer believe that which you believed before. The prior belief is what has created this situation. You expect that miracle to occur, because your belief in that miracle (or that shift in your perception) that belief is what enables that shift to occur. So you expect it to occur. Expect a miracle.

7.) **Repeat.** You then use this process repeatedly as necessary when your emotions trigger you to grow.

Question: Is emotional release a continuous process while on this planet?

MASTERS: Emotional release is a continuous process just as breathing is a continuous process. The expansion of energy is a continuous process. As you know, the energy of GOD is continually expanding. The process of emotional release is the vehicle for this expansion in a very deep way. Do not be as apprehensive that the emotions will always be as raw, or as painful, as they may seem initially. As you continually heal aspects of your consciousness, you no longer can create situations that would cause you severe deprivation, severe pain or severe suffering. Instead, you create small, simple and innocuous situations that would teach you where your energy needs to be aligned with unconditional love. So yes, it is a continuous process, but the process gets easier, and easier, and easier. We would also say that there is another side of emotional release that you may want to focus on as you learn and use this process more and more.

The other aspect of emotional release that you may choose to focus on is the release of wonderful emotions of joy, which many humans have not had much experience expressing as well. The emotions of joy, elation, anticipation, are all a part of the continuum as well. Do not suppress them. There may be times you feel an overwhelming joy. There maybe times when you feel an overwhelming "ah" due to the growing union that you have with the Infinite Intelligence. Do not be concerned about expressing these either. For their expression is just as necessary to facilitate your growth. And you will have more and more experiences of this wonderful exhilaration and joy that you will want, and need, to express. Now the reason you might feel uncomfortable about expressing these emotions is that they may be relatively unfamiliar to you, or you may feel that you might not be able to sustain an extended period of joy or bliss. And there is a part of your consciousness that may feel guilty that you are experiencing such bliss when you observe such pain around you. In these instances you must tell yourself that you are simply responsible only for yourself. And that other beings who have incarnated have chosen paths that will move them towards, and in alignment with unconditional love in a time and in a way that is ideal for them. So all is in divine order. Yet you cannot take responsibility for others. You can, and must, only have responsibility for yourself.

We would then relate this to the purpose of your incarnation on this plane. This plane, the earth plane, is an illusion. It is a theater in the round where your soul can observe the misperceptions that the soul has. The soul, through the human consciousness, can create the situations that are reflections of these misperceptions. Where you perceive yourself to be unlovable, you create situations that are not loving to you. Where you perceive yourself to be guilty, you create situations that would draw you to punishment. Through this creation on this canvass called earth, on this theater in the round called earth, on this illusion called earth where your human consciousness exists, you can see what you are creating and you can see how damaging it can be.

You can then see what you must do to change what you are creating. For the true you, the eternal you, the soul of you, the part of you that is connected, and has always been connected to GOD's unconditional love, is sitting in the audience in this theater in the round. The real you is watching this drama unfold, and screaming, and screaming, and screaming, "Don't go through that door again, there's a monster back there!" Eventually you hear. Eventually you choose not to go through the door. Eventually you choose to neutralize the monster. Eventually you choose to think differently, and therefore to create differently.

Eventually you choose to evolve yourself, and therefore you choose to help evolve the earth. Your purpose in being here is to do just that -- to evolve yourself -- to draw to yourself experiences of love, and light, and creativity instead of experiences of pain, and deprivation, and lack. You are doing so in a wonderful way, and therefore, transforming the theater in the round where pain has been created, into the theater in the round where reflections of love are created. In the process, GOD's light has been magnified, and that is your true purpose.

Now, there are many paths toward the awareness of unconditional love, the experience of unconditional love, and the simple ingestion, digestion and promulgation of unconditional love. There are as many ways to do this as there are individuals. **So your life path, in terms of specific vocations or activities, is simply the vocation and activity which brings you the most joy and seems the most effortless and fulfilling.** You should choose the vocation that makes you feel like you are absorbing more and more of your soul energy. In other words, the purpose that makes you feel right. Do not judge where you are in this process. Simply understand that where you are in this process is perfect for you, for it gives you the optimal opportunity to align yourself with GOD's unconditional love, which is the ultimate purpose of your existence.

Question: I feel confused about my situation because, as you have said, we need to sustain our being on this earth. Yet spirit seems to want me to keep re-exposing myself to situations that cause me pain. I don't understand how this fits into the pattern of things.

MASTERS: Yes, we will work with you and this question. You see there is a part of your consciousness that has evolved quite rapidly and quite wonderfully, and is truly, and definitely, and deeply aligned with the world of spirit. This part of you is so aligned with light that it feels uncomfortable around energies that are not vibrating in the same way, at the same level, or ingesting and moving out light at the same velocity. This part of the consciousness feels that it cannot survive in the environment where it is exposed to the energies of self-hatred and self-rejection that are around it as embodied in other individuals. The part of the consciousness that has evolved so greatly, so wonderfully, and so rapidly, fears that the surrounding consciousness would harm it. The basis of this fear is the subconscious memory of other times when the other incarnations where there was persecution, and ultimately suffering because you chose to embody and exhibit so much light. And so there is a fear and a feeling of separation. There is also a feeling that because so much of your soul's energy has been infused in your human energy and is vibrating with light, there is a desire for part of that soul's energy to return to the source.

The practical answer to your questions is as follows: The ultimately loving thing to do is not to subject yourself to suffering. There is no longer a need to suffer. There is a need to face your fears and neutralize them through the energy of light that you send to your workplace. You may ask this collective group of beings to send light to your workplace, and you may ask the collective consciousness of those who populate this space to send their energy to this workplace as well. We would see that in the next several weeks this will no longer be a dilemma for you. Protect yourself, and from a distance, send the light into the space so that the toxic physical environment (which is a reflection of your perception that the emotional environment there is toxic) and the environment becomes more neutralized.

You believe that you would be hurt or harmed there. The reason that you believe you would be hurt or harmed there is because you are different. The reason you are different is because you are vibrating at a different rate, with a different velocity and with different qualities than the predominant energy there. You have memories that in past lives, when you dared to be different in this way, you were hurt, maimed or killed. This did occur. But this was the past. This was an era where there was not enough light to sustain you. In the current time and space, there is enough light to sustain you, and you are working through old fears and misperceptions that this seemingly hostile environment would hurt you because it has in the past. What you must learn is that it will not hurt you. You have the power to neutralize it. And your task is to neutralize it.

There are times when you must do this from a distance, for you should not place yourself in harm's way - for that is not loving to you. But you are being stretched to call on the healing power within you, and the healing energy of those who surround you, both physically and spiritually, to help you with this process. And this will occur. And you will have peace in the next several weeks.

Author's Note

According to the Masters, "fear is the anticipation of the pain and suffering caused by guilt. Therefore, in order to eliminate fear from your life in a deeper way, it is important to eliminate the guilt that is the root cause of the fear." Since much of our consciousness is fear based, it is especially important to look closely at the guilt that is at the root of fear. This next section provides specific guidance on healing guilt.

Healing Guilt

We would talk to you now about guilt. This should be no surprise. The channel volunteered, on a level, to receive lessons in guilt that could be related in a timely way, so that the information that might otherwise seem esoteric, would be very real to you in a very specific and timely example.

The channel is about to accept a wonderful, wonderful gift from the universe (a new BMW Convertible). It is a gift of the channel's creation that has actually been in the channel's consciousness for ten years, and is coming to fruition. In order to receive this gift, there has been a continual opening of the channel to light. For as you know from your prior classes, the energy expands, and expands in light. The more light the energy field contains, the more able the being is to draw to him or her that which the being desires, because the being literally becomes magnetized to draw that to him or her. And the light of the being expands in its density, or lack of density because it is light, and its power to create and to draw to it its desires. So the channel, through many, many hours and work, opened his energy field to accept this wonderful gift which had been years in the making. However, through this process, and through the continual enlightenment that the channel receives, just as each of you receives continual enlightenment, more light was shown on other parts of the channel's consciousness and had to be recognized, realized and transformed as well.

The channel created several situations for this. One of which was a speeding ticket on the eve of receiving this gift because the channel, on some level felt guilty and undeserving, and therefore unable to and unready to accept this gift. Through this incident, the channel recognized the guilt and the feelings of unworthiness. The channel was triggered to not only recognize, but also to release the guilt. The channel was guided to transform the guilt through prayer energy work, and to heal that part of the consciousness that was not yet ready to accept such a wonderful gift. And if we say no more, you would now understand what we would say to you about guilt. But we would say more.

We would first talk about the origin of the feeling of guilt in the mass consciousness. As you know, you are individualized pieces of the totality that is the light of GOD. As individualized pieces of the totality that is the light of GOD, you are all unique. Yet you are not separate. However, you perceive yourselves as separate on some level. And through that perception of separation, you have created many manifestations of separation. And the "you" that we refer to now is the "you" of humanity, and those who inhabit the earth - the collective "you" - of the inhabitants of the earth.

You believe on some level that you are separate from each other, and also separate from GOD. You believed that as you emanated from the heart of GOD, you became separate from GOD. Part of you is not aware that your purpose was to find your way to express, to recreate the light of GOD, to magnify the light of GOD, and to explore and expand the light of GOD. You felt as if you were no longer as connected to the source. As you perceived other individualized expressions of wholeness of GOD, you perceived that some lingered closer to home, and others strayed further away. You perceived these separations, and you judged them. And you judged yourself negatively, because you were separate, or so you perceived. This judgment lodged deeply within the individualized and the collective consciousness, and manifested as guilt. As a feeling, or belief, that you were inherently flawed, or bad, or wrong because you feel, and felt, that you had strayed.

A parable that was given to humanity at one point in time was the parable of the Prodigal Son. You all, and once again this is the collective "you" of the mass consciousness that permeates and inhabits the earth now, You all have felt like prodigal children. You have carried this guilt. We would work with you not only with our words, but primarily with our energies, to release you and to continue a process of release from this guilt. What you need to know, intellectually. Is that **you are not, nor have you ever been separate from each other, or from the Light of GOD.**

You have not done wrong by moving in a spatial relationship that you would perceive to be outside the heart of GOD. You have done nothing wrong in moving in a way that you would perceive outside of the core and the heart of GOD. For you have done GOD's will. GOD's will in creating you, was to give you freedom, choice and power, was so that you could explore, expand, experiment and create. You have done just that, so you have done GOD's will. Therefore, there is no reason for you to feel guilty that you have strayed from the flock or that you have moved from the fold. You have done what has been in Divine Order for you to do. And you must understand this now at a very deep level. Therefore, guilt has no place in your energy field. It is a part of the illusion of separation which we are now working very ardently to dispel in your minds.

We now offer a prayer:

Mother/Father GOD, Creator, Sustainer, Giver of Life, we perceive that we are separate from Your Light. This perception is an error. We open ourselves to a correction of this perception now. This perception has caused us guilt. This guilt has created pain and suffering for us. We wish for this pain and suffering to stop now. Therefore, we open to a correction of our mis-perception. We open to the truth that we have never been separate from Your Light. For we are Your Light. We are not guilty for emanating from Your Light. We are innocent. We are not flawed for emanating from Your Light. We are perfect. We are innocent and we are perfect. We accept our innocence now. We accept our perfection now. And we release guilt, and any perception of our imperfection. AMEN.

Please remember to breathe as we send this healing energy through you. Collectively, your inner eye is opened to perceive what guilt need to be surrendered to the Light.

So we will work with you in a new way this evening, where we will give you visual images of the misperceptions that you will subsequently work with and heal to move out of your energy any guilt that might have dislodged by this Light. We will work primarily with your inner eye. We will also work with your other senses in stimulating them in this safe place. So we would ask you now to assume a meditative state. We would begin with three Aum's. We would now ask you to call up in your mind any information that you need to recognize where you are feeling guilty. We would have you say now:

⁂

The opposite of guilt is innocence. I am innocent. I will not create out of guilt. I will create only out of my innocence.

⁂

Now we would ask you to visually, or in whatever way you are comfortable, recreate the situation out of innocence. Feel the energy of transformation as it has transformed you in a very deep way. We will say that this transformation will continue over the several weeks. You would all step more deeply into the Kingdom of Heaven, which we will discuss now.

⁂

The Kingdom of Heaven is a place here on earth where you are fully aware of you divinity, and you are beginning to become masterful at creating with the aspect of yourself that is divine. In the Kingdom of Heaven, you begin to create a preponderance of experiences that are joyful, and uplifting, and positive and expansive.

In the Kingdom of Heaven, understand your power to uncreate that which no longer serves you, and to move through any depth in your consciousness where there is not yet the awareness of your GOD-ness and your goodness. This is a state of extended bliss that is becoming more and more prevalent with individuals on the earth who aspire to it, and who work with the concepts we discuss in classes like this. This is a realm that is not off limits to you. Indeed, many of you have stepped into this realm, only to step back in the earth plane. What we would say is that as you become more comfortable in this realm, it will be the realm of your primary existence. Where the vast, vast majority of your experiences are loving, and wonderful and blissful.

Do you understand this? [yes]
Do you feel you are deserving of this? [yes]
Do you desire this? [yes]

Then it shall be yours. You will, over the next several weeks, be shown aspects of your consciousness in a wonderfully loving way that will be transformed so that more and more of your consciousness is ready to observe and live in more and more of the Kingdom of Heaven. This channel entered into this space several years ago and continually became acclimated to a space of joy, bliss, expansiveness, peace, comfort, light, alignment and fullness. And he has made a home there. There are others that have also made a home there. You, too, are making a home there, and will continue this process. There will be more support for each and every one of you as all take each other more deeply into the Kingdom of Heaven just as you are supporting each other now. As you release the old beliefs that would keep you locked in a consciousness of pain and suffering while on earth, we are unlocking the door to the realm of heaven on the earth.

We would now open this session for any additional questions that you have on the subject matter that we covered, or any other areas that you would like to cover this evening.

Question: I need some assistance with the guilt issue, especially about the amount of weight I'm carrying on my body. I have grappled with this for a number of years. And since I have had it,

I've grappled with it, and with the guilt about it, and I need spirit's assistance in moving this.

MASTERS: Yes. We would relate to you the lesson, from the channel's consciousness that occurred earlier this week. The channel went on a diet for four hours. The channel chose a time and a lesson to move deeper into the realm of unconditional loving acceptance of himself. The channel also chose to start the diet on the morning after an evening where the channel did intense physical labor in his garden, and therefore, was sore. The channel also chose to start the diet the morning after an evening when the channel did not get adequate sleep over the weekend. Therefore, the channel chose to create a situation that made the channel miserable. Through experiencing this misery, the channel realized that the experience was not aligned with unconditional love because there is no misery in unconditional love. Through this realization, the channel learned that the channel would accept every part of himself completely and unconditionally.

The challenge that you give yourself is the challenge of the mass consciousness versus the consciousness of GOD. The consciousness of GOD does not judge, or rate, or berate, or see what you perceive as the imperfection of your weight. The consciousness of GOD sees only the weight of your light, which is quite heavy. The human consciousness, however, judges, and categorizes and denigrates based on the standards of perfection that are part of the illusion of human consciousness. And you must ask yourself, "Would you like to be immersed in the human consciousness, which is full of pain, and suffering, and denigration, and separation, and disharmony? Or would you like to move your consciousness to the consciousness of Heaven, where there is only perfection and innocence?" As you answer that question, you then understand that, as you move your consciousness out of the mass consciousness and into the consciousness of Heaven, you no longer judge yourself.

We would supplement this with the additional part of the process of moving into the Kingdom of Heaven wherein you do not substitute an excessive amount of anything for the light you desire. For your consciousness also shifts so that you know that you have all that you need, and you are ultimately and truly being fed by the light. Therefore, you need not overfeed your body to substitute for the light that you perceive as being withheld from you. So these two principles will work in tandem in a wonderfully magical way. You will accept yourself as you are.

You will move to a weight that is more self loving, for it would not in any way compromise the well being of the temple which holds you soul, or a growing majority of your soul, which is your body. So you will move to a weight that is more self loving in a wonderfully natural, organic and peaceful way as your consciousness moves more and more into a space that is more self loving in a wonderfully natural, wonderful and organic way.

We would also pluck from the consciousness the channel something that the channel is not aware of at that deep level yet. And that is, over the course of the last week, the channel has not been receiving the usual amount of caffeine that the channel had, at one point, believed that he needed. And there has been no deleterious effect. Because the channel is slowly, peacefully and organically replacing that which he perceived that he received from caffeine with light, which is the true source of that which the body craved through the use of caffeine.

Reassure yourself, nor beat your body into submission, for all will occur in its wonderfully right time and Divine way. And we bless you.

Question: I was wondering if Spirit could give some assistance with this issue. I seem to be able to get stuck in depression in a way that I find that prayer, and meditation and emotional release really doesn't touch. And I find it difficult to get out of that. The reason to get out of that is that I feel that I am unproductive. I'm unhappy when that happens. I was wondering if you could provide some clarity and direction on that.

MASTERS: Yes we shall. What we recommend for you on a physiological level is more physical exercise during these times. You see, there is no organic or physical component to what you perceive as a malady. That would be brought more into balance with physical exercise. We would also say that part of your processes in this lifetime is to "slough off" eons of mistreatment that you have received as a soul, as an eternal being. Part of that process is not known consciously by you, but subconsciously is being done, and manifests in what we would call "slow downs" of your energy. Understand that this is a natural process. What happens with you is that you sometimes have difficulty expressing a deep, deep anger from those eons of suffering because you cannot put your finger on the exact cause. Therefore, when you cannot attribute the anger to an exact cause, you hold the energy of anger and focus it inward in a subconscious way. And this is depression. Through the physical exercise that is suggested, you begin to touch with the awareness of anger, and you release the anger, even though you needn't be aware at all times of what generates the anger. This is part of your process.

You have chosen a very ambitious task in this life, which is to move through eons of old-held feelings into a realm of wonderment. And you are doing wonderfully in this process. It presents challenges such as this for you. For you are doing what we would say is a "cram course." The channel, and many in this room, also chose "cram" courses at this time. You chose what may seem to be a difficult existence because on the level of your soul, you know that there is enough light on earth to support you. So also be aware, and assured, that there is light supporting you.

Also be aware, and assured, that we are guiding you in a very meticulous way through this process. We are walking you through this process.

And we would like to offer you this prayer:

I have not gotten where I want to be in this life from my human perspective. Bur from my Divine perspective I am in the perfect place. I am where I need to

be. For I am in a place that would draw me deeper into the heart of GOD. AMEN.

Question: I want to say thank you so very much for this message. I think that this is one that I will be soaking up quite a bit. So I just wanted to thank you for that, I don't know that I've had the opportunity yet, to at least to say it out loud. Did you know I was thinking about this?

The other thing is I was working at this earlier today. I've been working hard at trying to release a lot of things, and a lot emotions and issues, and discard thoughts that are just erroneous, and that I choose not to believe anymore, and I want to believe all these wonderful things. And I do! And I affirm them. How long....I don't mean to be impatient, but I feel like, "is once enough?" How long do I need to keep asking? Is it wrong to want to...well, you know...GOD knows what I want!

MASTERS: We would draw your attention to a lecture that we offered previously, and a portion of the lecture was entitled "repeat." For when you affirm, and when you pray, and when you state your misperceptions, you in a sense are telling GOD; but in another sense, you are telling yourself. You are convincing each level and each layer of consciousness, and your collective experience. And by your collective experience, we say the collection of experiences that you have had as an individualized expression of GOD's perfection. So each time you do this, you tell not GOD, for GOD already knows. You tell yourself. And that is why it is important to continue. Because "yourself" has many dimensions, many layers and many experiences. And "yourself" must be convinced, at very deep layers, that this truth is the only truth.

Conquering Fear

It is our honor and our pleasure to work with you in this way. WE are always pleased when you open yourselves to our light in this way, and we are always pleased when more humans open themselves to this light. For this is our task to fulfill. And the more you are, and the more open the earth becomes, because it has more conduits for this light, the easier it becomes for us to fulfill our task of enlightenment. We would commend you all, first of all, on your individual ministries. And we would explain this.

Each of you is a vessel of light. Each of you contributes to the sum total of light on the planet. As you continue opening, you continue being able to channel the light of healing and the light of transformation to those people, to those events, and to those things that are in need of transformation. Ultimately this heals the planet and moves the planet on its path of evolution in a wonderfully productive (instead of destructive) way. Yes, we allude to the earth changes that some of you fear, and that many of you understand have been predicted. These earth changes are not going to be as severe as they have been predicted. Each of you, along with countless others, have opened to the light of healing in such a way that you help bring more and more light to the planet. So that the drastic and cataclysmic changes that have been predicted in the past do not have to manifest in such a drastic and cataclysmic way. Therefore, you need not let these predictions cause you further fear.

The first step in working with this fear is understanding that it is simply a coping mechanism that has been developed over time, due to the misperception that love was not present, due to the lack of awareness of love's presence. So as a simple misperception, it can be corrected quite simply, and its manifestations can be corrected quite simply. So you should not feel like you have to run a marathon with this. Understand that you may invoke the Grace of GOD. Through your becoming aware of your fears, and continually releasing them in prayer, you transform your fear so that your energy field no longer vibrates in any way with this fear. Then, you live with more peace, and more comfort, and more joy.

The first thing for you to understand is not judge fear. You become aware of fear by asking yourself in any given situation, "How do I feel? Do I feel at comfort, at ease, and at peace? Or do I feel tense, apprehensive and nervous?" When you exhibit the latter, you are exhibiting outgrowths, or signs, of fear. You can then ask, "Why do I feel fear?" As you ask, "Why do I feel fear?" you get an answer. The answer most probably will be related to the specific situation that causes you fear. So you then must go deeper and ask again, "In this situation which causes me fear, why do I feel fear?" You will get an answer that goes more deeply into the realms of your consciousness. You continually repeat this process until you get to the core reason that you are feeling fear in that situation. Then you use the process of emotional release that we described previously to release the fear and transform it. As a result, that part of your energy is no longer vibrating out of fear. In other words, that part of your energy which was unaware of love's presence is once again aware of love's presence.

Question: First I would like to say thank you to the group for the questions tonight, and especially thank you for the answers. I'd also like to say something that I said to another member after my first night here, which was, "It seems like committees work better on your side than down here!" I wasn't here for the first several sessions. And I've read over the transcripts about the emotional release. Part of me feels like I sort of understand, theoretically, but I was hoping that if you could perhaps review that a little bit, maybe I'd get a better understanding of how to go about the process.

MASTERS: In fairness to others, we will briefly synopsize the efficacy of emotional release, for that is what is most important for you to understand. You see, your energy field through eons of experiences of difficulty, pain and suffering, gathers within it places that do not yet accept the love and light of GOD, and do not yet clearly let that flow through. As you become more enlightened, and as the light touches these places and exposes them, the light unleashes those blocked energies. By acknowledging and becoming aware of the root cause of those blocked and nonmoving energies through emotional release, you heal a part of your consciousness. You then clear more and more of your energy field to absorb, hold and disperse light. And you are moved more effortlessly on your life's path. You have been conditioned as a human **not** to release emotion. For there is a view that it would upset the social consciousness.

Therefore, you must release your emotions in a way that is not disruptive. Therefore, through your prayers and meditation, you create a safe space for emotional release where you may have the emotions, instead of bottling them up. As you see your emotions objectively, you can see them as Divine tool that help you to align every aspect of your consciousness with the love and light of GOD.

So you have the emotion, you honor the emotion, you honor yourself, without thinking that this is a bad thing, or that you are a spiritual person and therefore should not experience this bad thing. Instead, you must understand that it is an objective process that leads to your growth, and is therefore wonderful and perfect. You then release the emotion in whatever way seems appropriate. You may use your voice to vent your emotions, you may strike a pillow, or you may let yourself cry. You then ask, "What awareness, what misperception, did I hold that caused this event, which caused this emotion?" And in this place of peace, you receive the answer you need. And with that answer you understand your misperception, so you pray that it be moved into an alignment with GOD, and through prayer a transformation takes place. A miracle, also known as a shift in your perception, then occurs. The miracle is that the misperception no longer exists, and the **truth** is embedded in your consciousness in place of the illusion that has just been released. So through the process of emotional release, you make room for more light and more truth by expelling that which is no longer aligned with truth. So you increase your own alignment with the light. And you continue this process more, and more, and more as the light continually flows through as you relieve the blockages to absorbing, sustaining, and dispersing light as part of you're your Divine plan. We hope this brief synopsis helps you to understand the process more fully.

Question: I feel sort of like two people in a way, one of trust and one of fear.

MASTERS: Yes. Again, you see that your soul energy is merging with your human energy. Which do you think is your soul energy? We are guiding your path in a very meticulous way, as you are each on a path that is open to our light and the light of our Creator. Be not afraid. Simply call on our light, and the light of our Creator as you need. Be blessed.

Question: After you talked last week about fear, and after I started going through the transcript, I started asking myself, "What have I really been afraid of?" And one thing that keeps coming to mind, and I still cannot understand on a consciousness level is, when my grandmother was dying and I was driving my mother, and myself and my uncle back and forth to the hospital, I had such an intense fear, not of driving, but of expecting to see something jump out from the woods that I would never forget. Could you please explain that because it just eludes me. I still cannot comprehend where that came from. Because I can still feel the fear when I go back to Italy and drive at night.

MASTERS: This association is deep. For you associate the driving with death. And the true fear is the fear of death, which is associated with driving, and fear that in death the soul is annihilated. And for fear in death there is a hell and there is suffering. You are opening to a new reality now. And this new reality releases the fear caused by the subconscious illusion that death is equated with suffering, and hell, and final endings. That is the simplest answer that we may transmit to with the remaining energies.

And we thank you, each and everyone, for your presence, for your willingness to open to the light of your Creator, and therefore facilitate the work of bearing the light on the planet. For that is not work, that is joy, and natural, and **you!** For that is your essence. Be blessed and be in light. **Live your light.**

MASTERS: Please repeat the following prayer:

Mother/Father GOD, I release to your light all guilt, all perception of separation. I open to union with Your Light. I open to a full, loving acceptance for myself so that Your full, loving acceptance of me may be made manifest through every aspect of my life. I ask You to heal my mind of the guilt that it holds. I ask You to heal my body of the guilt that it holds. I ask You to heal my energy of the guilt that it holds. I ask you to heal my soul of the guilt that it holds. I open to Your light now in a deep way. And I ask for a deep transformation so that the guilt that has lived within me is now released to Your Light. AMEN.

Question: I am finding it difficult, not only to function physically, but mentally and spiritually as well.

MASTERS: You were not responsible for anything that occurred previously in your life. For **you** were not **you** then. **You** are **you** now. You are continually transforming yourself into a **new** you every day. Every day you are becoming more and more Light. And everyday you are renewed with this Light. So you need not carry any vestiges of the past as you move forward. For these vestiges are no longer relevant. You are learning, through this experience, to release guilt. For you are learning of the pain and suffering that it causes. You are learning that guilt is not of Light. Therefore you must release it as you ascend into Light in the way that you desire. There are many beings of Light who are helping you through this process. There are many beings of Light who are actually walking you through this process.

You do not have to suffer. Would you repeat that please. **I do not have to suffer. I will not suffer. I cannot suffer for I am a being of Light. And my Light knows no suffering.** And we would say that you may have more to release. You may want to release your frustration, anger, fear. You are safe. As you choose to release it, you let our Light move through you more deeply. And we will all send healing energy to this sister through the use of AUM. Know that your suffering will not continue.

Question: Is that on a physical level as well?

MASTERS: Yes. As above, so below. What occurs on the plane of the expanded consciousness and raised, or heightened, or speeded vibration also occurs below on the plane of the slowed or reduced vibration and consciousness, which is the earth plane. As above, so below. We would suggest that you paraphrase, or repeat whole, the prayers that were given you tonight so that you may facilitate your own healing. This veil will be lifted...this cloud will be removed from your energy, and you will be whole again soon.

Question: The work that I did last weekend surrounding Mother's Day. Is that useful in this release process?

MASTERS: Yes. You see, your guilt stems from this issue. And it may not seem at this time that was useful, in truth it was. For you see, many times when healing occurs, it seems as if things are getting worse instead of better. But what is truly happening at these times is that **all** that must be surrendered to the Light that is moving through you so that it may be transformed, and so that which is deeply held comes up for transformation.

What you must understand is that it only comes up when you are ready, and strong enough, and have enough support from the Light that dwells within you to strengthen and heal you, and help you to release it. And you have drawn enough Light, and enough strength and enough support that you will move through this. For GOD is moving you through this.

Question: Even after all that work, it just seems like...it felt like the emptiness of Mother's Day was like a punishment no matter what I did. <the participant refers to her estrangement from her children>

MASTERS: You are not in any way being punished. Remember again that you are not responsible for what happened then. For **you** were not **you** then. Therefore you have transformed yourself out of judgment of yourself. You have transformed yourself out of a prior existence. Therefore, you need not feel guilt about it, or manifest that guilt by perceiving that you are being punished. Know that you are being loved, that you are being accepted, that you are being supported. For you are lovable and acceptable, and deserving of support.

The process of release that you are working with now is, and will continue to be, quite useful for you. There are many who love you, and respect you, and revere you. You serve, and will serve, in the capacity as a mother to many. So you do not in any way have to feel like you are less than whole, or perfect, or acceptable because a role that you have chosen to play in this life does not seem to be fulfilled at this time because of estrangement. You **are** fulfilling a divine task. You will, and you do, have the opportunity to give and experience the same unconditional love that is associated with motherhood. And the key here is unconditional love. For it comes without condition. So you see, as you release the need for validation, because of the role you feel that you have not fulfilled, you understand your true validity. For that role is truly being fulfilled. And that role is the role of bearing unconditional love, which you do wonderfully. You receive unconditional love wonderfully. So you are whole. And your wholeness is not contingent on your children's perception of you. There is no need for guilt.

We would also say that we do understand the jumble of emotions and the depth of pain that you feel and release to our Light now.

❧❧❧❧

MASTERS: We would say to you please continue to breathe. Even when life seems at its darkest, it is simply an opportunity for you to open to the Light that you know is at the other end of the spectrum from darkness. For in experiencing the darkness, you appreciate, revere, call out for and open to the Light in a deeper way. For the Light then penetrates the darkness and transforms it until all is Light, and only Light. So be not afraid of those darkest parts of the self which are being transformed into light as you are ready to transform them. For the end result is a being resplendent in Light while here on the earth plane.

CHAPTER 8.
THE DIVINE NATURE OF RELATIONSHIPS

Question: This week I have been presented with many opportunities to judge myself and others negatively. And this is an area that I have worked on for years and it still persists. Would you please tell me why, and how I could transform this area of my life?

MASTERS: Yes we would. We would first send you the healing that you have asked for on the level of your soul. The reason that these opportunities for growth have come up for you has been to enable you to move out of this karmic patterning into more peace. So these activities brought this karmic patterning into focus, and you have asked for this patterning to be transformed. We would lead you in a prayer of transformation. We would ask you to repeat the following prayer.

I understand that I am seeing reflections of myself in every person, in every being and in every situation that I create. I am seeing reflections of myself that I would judge, that I would find unacceptable, that I would see these as unacceptable because I perceive that GOD sees parts of me as unacceptable. I perceive that GOD judges me. I now know that this is false. GOD does not judge me in any way. GOD only loves me. GOD created in me the perfect and innocent image of GOD's light. I

ntain GOD's light. In GOD's light I am innocent. In GOD's light I am perfect. In GOD's light I am full. Therefore I am not lacking in any way and I no longer need to fear judgment. I no longer need to judge myself. Therefore I no longer need to judge aspects of my consciousness that are reflected to me. I now desire inner peace. I now desire that misperceptions and judgments that do not cause me peace be eliminated from my thought processes now. I ask that the light of GOD heal my mind from all needs to judge from all needs to separate others from me. I ask for peace. I expect peace. I accept peace. I have peace. And so it is. AMEN.

Question: What is the nature of a so-called "good" marriage for two people that are on the spiritual path? It seems as though it would be something more than spiritual utilitarian. I would like you to comment.

MASTERS: We are working to understand, and empathize with the intent of your question versus the literal statement. We would first say that there is no "good" marriage, or no "bad" marriage. We would begin by reviewing the purpose of a relationship. The purpose of any relationship, up to and including, and past a relationship which results in marriage, is to help each individual to grow. Each partner in a relationship reflects to the other partner a portion of the consciousness that must be seen to assess its alignment with unconditional love, or its misalignment with, unconditional love. When there is an awareness, there is an opportunity for healing and realignment. If that opportunity is taken, then the soul grows. That is the purpose of any relationship. We will illustrate this with a more mundane relationship, such as you and the elevator operator, or the gas station attendant.

In an interaction like that, your task, if you choose to accept it, is to perceive the light in that individual, and acknowledge the light in the individual, bless the light within that individual and move forward. For as you bless, perceive and acknowledge the light within that individual, you are in essence blessing, and acknowledging, and perceiving the light within yourself because he is your reflection. As you do that, you nurture that light, and it grows, and grows, and grows until you are **only** light.

This composite person, the person in the service industry, has a similar task to you. The human mind, which has been steeped in the human consciousness, sees things in terms of separation and hierarchy. And as a result of this, the person in the service capacity might misperceive a lack because they feel that they are not at a place on the hierarchy that is deserving. As you acknowledge their light and they acknowledge yours, you move that person, and that person allows himself, to move into a place where they see themselves only as light, and not as one that is lacking. So in a simple example like that you see the Divine purpose of a relationship.

In an extended example, which constitutes a marriage, there are many, many opportunities and dimensions. We do not judge, so we would not categorize, or stratify, as "good" or "bad." We would only say that as it challenges you, and helps you, and catalyzes you to grow, then the relationship is fulfilling its Divine purpose and plan. When it does not, the relationship is not helping you to fulfill your divine purpose or plan. If it is not, your task is to assess if this is a time of rest, if this is a dormant bulb waiting to be replanted, re-fertilized so it will grow again, or if the tree has fulfilled its purpose, and therefore will no longer have a purpose. This is what we would say.

You are continuing to receive lessons, and reflections, and opportunities for growth; and as you recognize this purpose, you understand more about yourself. And you bring more of yourself into awareness. We hope that we have been able to address your question in a way that is comfortable for you. We hope that we have interpreted both the literal and the other intent of your question. If you would like to ask a follow up question, or rephrase your question, you may do so.

Question: The part when you said something about recognizing the GOD-light in the other person, that seemed to have the post potential for bearing fruit in the relationship. I guess I just am experiencing a deep longing for something more.

MASTERS: In other words you want a physical relationship. In this case, the soul, or the spirit, is moving ahead of the physical, and the physical must catch up. You experienced this recently in another dimension as a result of your trip. And when you returned, you and other colleagues experienced illness in a very interesting way, which was the body's needing to catch up with the aura, and you understood this. By the same token, you are now able to relate with others from a place of more light as your individual light has grown. This expanded ability has triggered a longing for the experience of a heart felt relationship on the earth plane. In other words, for the body to catch up with the spirit once again.

Or should we say more broadly and more effectively, the physical to catch up with the spiritual. So we would say to you that your task now is to hold in you mind that which you desire, state it to the universe, visualize it, affirm it, pray for it, release yourself from any demands that it come in a specific form, and you will have more peace with this. Do you understand?

Question: The last part I understood. But I wasn't quite sure what you were referring to when you said, which physical is it that's catching up?

MASTERS: Your experience on the physical realm is trying to catch up with your experience on the spiritual realm. And that is what we refer to.

Question: I believe it's probably a past life situation, and confirm this for me, why I have a fear of commitment.

MASTERS: Yes. We would say to you with all due love, honor and respect, that it is a past life issue, it is a present life issue, and it is possible a future life issue. But it is truly a wonderful gift.

Without going into intimate details that would not be appropriate for this forum, we would say to you, that in order to understand your seeming inability to commit, you must understand a deeper truth about commitment.

Commitment, in the sense of the word as you use it, is a commitment to be with another individual "come hell or high water." Commitment has connotations of being in bondage. It truly is a form of bondage that keeps the soul from being free to experience whatever the soul must experience at any given time for its growth. You see, there are many types of relationships, and all are holy relationships.

Relationships are created to offer you a mirror image of your awareness. For what you see in any relationship is an aspect of your awareness embodied. The fleeting relationships may show you an aspect of your consciousness, or your awareness. And you may choose to accept that part of your consciousness and ask what are you to learn from it, and how can you align it with the Light. Or you may reject it. You are then shown it again. You are always shown parts of your consciousness in order that you may align them with the consciousness of GOD. The less fleeting relationships also are there to show you other aspects of your consciousness so that you may examine them and see where they are aligned with light, and where they are not. Longer term or special relationships are also there for that purpose.

However, those long-term relationships may give many lessons. At times they may have given you all the lessons that you require. If the long-term relationship has given you all the lessons that you require, or that you may glean from it, yet you stay in it out of a commitment, you are not working in accordance with your soul's greater purpose, which is to continually expand. For you are not giving yourselves an opportunity to expand more, and more. You are locked into a nonmoving energy pattern. You do understand that the purpose of any nonmoving energy pattern is to release itself from non-movement, and to expand so the Light may expand. Therefore, what we say is that you're seemingly difficult time committing has to do with a subconscious understanding of the holiness of every relationship.

The other part of your seeming inability to commit has to do with a certain reluctance to face certain aspects of your consciousness as they are shown to you in reflection by another individual. Your difficulty at this time is facing them, for you judge them to be unworthy, and you judge them to be undesirable, when in fact they are wonderfully desirable. For they are wonderful tools for your growth and you need not judge them. You now have an expanded understanding of the purpose of any relationship, either a fleeting relationship, or a more substantial relationship. Understand that all of these relationships are holy, and are tools for your soul's growth and evolution and union, and alignment with unconditional love and light, then you may move forward without fear for you know that what you are doing is evolving the soul in this endeavor. For you are evolving the soul in every endeavor.

Part of the fear also comes when a relationship is of a long-term nature and is not used as a tool for evolving the soul, but is used as a tool for usurping the Light of another. Then there is always a fear that that source of Light would be cut off. And therefore, there is a fear of involvement. For there is a fear that the involvement would ultimately lead to pain if the involvement were to end. And we would explain this further.

You see, at a subconscious level the human being understands that light is the source of life. When the human being comes into incarnation, the human being receives the life force from the parents. When the human is born, the human being receives all that it needs from the parents to sustain it. As a helpless infant, if something is withheld, the human child believes that it may not survive. The child is totally dependent on the parents and as a result, the child has shifted its perception. The child misperceives that the outside force of the parent is the source of what they need to survive as opposed to the GOD source within them that is connected to the GOD source that they perceive outside of them. So there has been what we would call a "transference or a substitution". In truth, the Light that resides within a human is connected to the Light that emanates from the source, and that this light is what is needed for life. Instead, the human being perceives and believes that what they need for their sustenance instead comes from another human vessel, their parents.

This misperception that what is needed comes from outside the human being, then is transferred as the human being progresses. It is transferred to peer groups during adolescence, which is why peer groups seem to have so much power over teenagers. This transference then migrates to external forces such as means of economic survival, or jobs, and/or to other individuals who appear as surrogate parents (spouses, dates, etc.). This transference continues throughout the human's life.

There is always the underlying fear that the source, as it is perceived by the human, will be cut off. This is why most humans live in a consciousness of fear. The human does not perceive that the source is everlasting, and that the source is the life force within them that is connected to the life force of GOD, and therefore is eternal. So this misperception is the genesis of a great deal of fear. It is why one individual may try to control another individual through the use of shame, guilt, manipulation, or other forms of emotional blackmail. It is why co-dependencies are set up in relationships, because the individuals do not believe that GOD is the source, and the GOD within them is connected to GOD at all times. Instead they believe that the source is their partner and thus they become co-dependent on their partner. And so the dramas ensue.

The dramas are actually tools for making the individuals aware of the truth that the other individual, or individuals, with whom they are involved are not the sources of their sense of self worth, but GOD is the source of all that they need. And when they manifest enough painful, tenuous or fear-filled relations to make that shift, they will. So all relationships are holy, for they move the individual back to the ultimate relationship with the One. And when you are ready to face that truth, and live that truth, and relate with that truth, then you can see the relationship not as a threatening thing that must be avoided. Instead you will then see a relationship as a wonderful tool that is a gift that you give yourselves so that you may find your souls.

Question: I have a question about a co-dependent relationship. One person spirals, and hopes that the other person will come along. I am feeling frustration and anger because I do not want to go along with this person's downward spiral.

MASTERS: Yes, you have heard part of your answer. Sending light to the person opens a door that the person may or may not choose to come through. We would offer additional insights. There is nothing you can do to control this person's choices, actions or reactions. You can only control you. Therefore, in order to give yourself peace of mind, you might choose to release yourself from any investment in the person's reactions. You might choose to give yourself the gift of peace NO MATTER WHAT. You might choose to open yourself in a relationship in a way that you desire to be served in a relationship and then leave the rest up to GOD without demanding that the relationship come from this individual. You see GOD has an infinite number of ways to serve you and give you your heart's desires. By giving GOD permission to serve you through an infinite number of channels in an infinite number of ways, you are "untying GOD's hands". You then optimize the probability of creating and receiving your heart's desires.

If you choose to disengage, you must do so without guilt. You must realize that the other person has made choices and is a willing participant in this drama, but you cannot be responsible for the choices that the other person makes. If this person chooses not to come along, but you must move forward, it is as if you are in the 5th grade and the person is in the 2nd grade. It may be challenging for you two to relate to each other as much, because your experiences are very different. However, you can meet in the playground for recess from time to time.

We would then provide some additional background for you on the nature of relationships. Each relationship is holy because each relationship gives you an opportunity to see a reflection of a part of your consciousness. You can either accept this reflection of your consciousness or you can reject it. However, as you know, when you reject a part of your consciousness, it becomes difficult to vibrate in complete unconditional loving acceptance. Yet accepting a part of your consciousness does not mean accepting it in a way that is detrimental to you. Accepting this part of your consciousness means that when you see this part of your consciousness, you can heal it within yourself without needing to create pain and suffering for yourself.

As this relates to the other individual, they may or may not choose to heal or grow. If they do not choose to heal or grow, you cannot lose yourself in an effort to save them. You cannot lose the peace and growth that you have experienced. In other words, if there is another individual who is sinking in quicksand, you cannot rescue them by jumping into the quicksand with them, you can only rescue them by standing on firm solid ground and throwing them a lifeline. They then must choose to catch the lifeline and pull themselves out of the quicksand. If they choose not to grab the lifeline, they will stay in the quicksand.

You can work with this individual with compassion. The human mind sometimes has difficulty accepting the truth that each individual is responsible for themselves and that each individual creates the situations in their lives in a way that is ultimately for their greatest good. Some of the experiences may seem to be challenging or painful. However, even those experiences that are challenging or painful are for the individual's greatest good because when these experiences create enough pain, they force the individual to choose a different set of experiences. This process ultimately enables the individual to make choices that reflect unconditional love --- unconditional love of self, and faith in GOD's unconditional love. And this is the purpose of life on the earth plane – to become re-connected with the energies of unconditional love.

Question: This question concerns strategies in dealing with passive/aggressive individuals. I have a difficult time with this kind of personality, to the point where I don't really love these people very much (which is horrible to say). I wondered if Spirit could help us with that. The second question might be related. It's how to get beyond worrying. My mother and I are great worriers. My grandmother was the worrier of all worriers, and we decided it was definitely a gene that we inherited. But we both seem to care a lot. And the adjective for me that my mother gave for me was that I tend to "stew" over things. She may say this of me, but my mother is the "crock pot". And so we wondered what you could say about that, Spirit.

MASTERS: It is truly a situation where the crock pot is calling the kettle black. [The group laughs at this retort] There is a healing energy in laughter. There is an emotional release in laughter. There is a cathartic nature in laughter that heals and brings you back to balance.

We would begin with your first question. Any individual that you see is showing you a reflection of your own consciousness that you can accept or reject. Your task is to accept all aspects of your consciousness. And those that you find distasteful, understand why you find them distasteful. The reason that you find them distasteful is that they do not seem to be in keeping with your understanding of perfection. Your task is to love yourself completely and unconditionally. And those parts of your consciousness that are reflected to you that you find distasteful are those that you do not love completely and unconditionally. So your task is to ask: "What am I to learn in this situation with this seemingly passive/aggressive person?" You will be given the answer. You will be shown where you are not accepting yourself, and you will be shown the misperception that your lack of acceptance is based on. Then, if you choose, you will heal that misperception. As a result, you will no longer need to immerse yourself in relationships with passive/aggressive people.

Generally, the passive-aggressive person simply needs to be loved, and their action is a cry for love. However, this cry for love may be troublesome because it tries to draw love to it through subtle forms of manipulation. The other person resents these subtle forms of manipulation and the passive/aggressive person does not reach the goal of receiving love. As a result both parties are frustrated because both parties feel unloved through the process. Your task is to look at the fact that you feel unloved when you feel manipulated. As you look to GOD as the source of love, and as you know that love can come through an infinite number of conduits on the earth plane, you no longer need to set up the expectation that this person send you love in the specific way that you demand. You can then accept this person with compassion, because you are no longer dependent on this person as a source of your love.

When you treat this person with compassion, and send them love that you get directly from the heart of GOD, you have healed yourself, the person and the situation – and that is why this situation has been created. This process works for all difficult people.

Speaking of immersing ones self in a crock pot (and we will call you our loving crock pot of light), worry is a manifestation of fear. Fear is a manifestation of the mis-perception that GOD does not love you, and therefore would punish you. As you experience more and more of GOD's light personally through prayer and meditation, you move out of the place of fear because your experience of GOD is not an experience of fear. As you do this more and more, you worry less and less. For you know that GOD only wants to give to you, and love you, and bring you home in alignment with the consciousness of GOD.

Question: On Monday evening my husband and I had a rather one-sided conversation that was brought on from taxes on the surface, and I believe that it had a very deeper meaning. And I think we both learned something from it, but I don't think either one of us learned anything consciously. I think it was learned more on a soul level. Can you give me some insight on that?

MASTERS: Yes. We will of course give you the insight that has the greatest applicability to all, yet preserves your privacy. And what happened here was the subconscious balance, and the resolution of a deeper issue that is not all necessarily from this lifetime. In other lifetimes there have been (and we are giving the channel the image of a wrestling match) there have been power struggles. We would then call you our dear Hulk Hogan of light. The interaction in this situation on a subconscious level was designed to bring older, simmering memories of these power struggles into balance. What you must trust through this process is that you and this person have brought deeper-seated subconscious energies more into balance through this balance.

What this means for all of you is that **many times an issue is not what it appears to be at the surface. There are deeper issues going on at the level of the infinite experience of the soul, and those too are being resolved.** So trust the process to heal whatever must be healed...that which is known, and that which is unknown. And when you release, release that which is known and that which is unknown.

Question: We went through how we create our reality in doing visualization and prayer. And so when we have a certain goal, or effective lifestyle that we would like to obtain, and our significant other, or other specific relationship that we share a lot of time with, has their course set in a different direction, who wins? How does it match when both parties are creating something completely different, and yet they will affect the other by choice of lifestyle. And I'll be very specific so the group understands. I've been trying to send my husband a large amount of healing to help his physical body, and his emotional state of tension, and help him open more comfortably to spiritual aspects. And he is doing everything the opposite! He is eating everything that he can possibly eat that is terribly wrong for him, he is not exercising, he's not sleeping. He really wants nothing to do with spirit. And he is heading in a completely different direction from what I am trying to send him in. So where does it cross?

MASTERS: We would begin with your question, "who wins?" And we would also continue with our loving analogy with you before, where we lovingly referred to you as Hulk Hogan in a wrestling match. For you see, there is nothing to win, and there is no struggle necessary. We would also refer to a response we gave to an individual who was trying to send healing to her brother in a prior session. For you see, you are doing what you are needing to do. You are working with yourself. You are doing what your human mind believes that it should do for another individual. For your human mind feels that it should, and must, take responsibility for another individual's life, almost to the point of wanting to take control of the other individual's life. Do you understand how this dynamic might set up a subtle test of wills? What we would reinforce for you this evening is that there is always free will. When you send another person light, that person chooses to either accept that light and use it now, or perhaps later. And if that person uses the light, it is there for that person. If that person does not choose to use that light, it is added to the reservoir of light that exists on the earth for healing and transformation.

Now in a practical sense, this person is a reflection of part of your consciousness. Part of your consciousness, of course, identifies and is rooted on the earth plane. Part of your consciousness fears that it would be destroyed as it moves through a path of transformation. Part of your consciousness does not yet understand that it is not being destroyed or eliminated, it is simply being transformed. So you are receiving a reflection of the part of your consciousness that is resistant. You are also receiving a wonderful lesson in learning about free will, your free will and the free will of others. You are also learning more about self-responsibility.

Try to not see this as a wrestling match, or as a test of wills, or a game to be won or lost, but to see it as it truly is: As an opportunity for you to see the parts of your consciousness that may be resistant to the light that you are drawing to you now, and to work with yourself and your own consciousness. It is a chance to accept that part of your consciousness, which is resistant. It is your chance to caress it, to love it, to cherish it, to embrace it, to be patient with it, to be loving with it, to give it the time it needs to experience what it needs to experience. Then when it chooses no longer to experience conflict, it is ready to accept transformation.

As you work with yourself in this way, you will find that your inner resistance lessens, and the reflection of that inner resistance is no longer troubling to you. You then have understood that the lesson is a lesson of self-responsibility, and you will have understood that each individualized expression of GOD's perfection has free will, and you will have realized that there is nothing to control, there is only that which wants to be received, and that is the Light of GOD.

Author's Comment

Generally in a context such as this, the Masters will also give another way see the situation so that we know that GOD is the ultimate source of all. They generally use a phrase called "Untying GOD's Hands", which means giving GOD permission to serve you in an unlimited number of ways and through an unlimited number of sources. This concept is based on the fact that we often have very specific demands based on our limited human perspective. These very specific demands do not take into consideration that truth that GOD is unlimited, and can provide our heart's desires in an unlimited number of ways. In essence we tie GOD's hands by giving GOD permission to serve us only in very narrow, predetermined ways. For example, a friend desperately wanted a baby but demanded that it be a little boy (she remembered how much trouble she had given her own mother). She had severe difficulty getting pregnant until the day she told GOD – "I want a child, I don't care what gender it is". Almost immediately, she became pregnant because in essence, she "untied GOD's hands".

Very often, we tie GOD's hands when sending out the request for a relationship. Often we want the relationship to come in a specific way, through a specific person at a specific time under specific circumstances. When sending out a request of this nature, it is helpful to be specific. However, when we send out this request, we should also try to untie GOD's hands by ending the request with the phrase "This or something better", which gives the Light of GOD permission to serve us in an unlimited number of ways. This simple phrase gives the Light of GOD permission to serve us in ways that we don't even dream of with our limited human minds.

The concept of "Untying GOD's Hands" also helps us to see that GOD is the source of our unlimited abundance, and GOD's abundance can be given to us through a number of different ways. Therefore, we do not have to be enslaved to a limited notion of who or what can bring us lasting peace, because we ultimately know that this peace comes from GOD, and can shine through an unlimited number of conduits on the earth plane. This simple understanding can alleviate so much pain and suffering, fear, self doubt and belief in lack that I thought it was well worth inserting in this context.

CHAPTER 9. THE DIVINE NATURE OF SEXUALITY

Many greetings and blessings to you from the world of reality. It is with joy, and pleasure, and with honor, and humility that we serve you in this way. We add the element of humility, for we are humbled at this opportunity. This is a purposeful humility in that we want to convey to you that we are your peers, for you are also Masters. You are Masters in the making.

You have accepted a very challenging task with courage. The task that you have accepted with courage is the task of humanity. The task you have accepted is the task of merging your higher selves with your human selves through the experiences that you create on the earth plane. Fulfilling this task triggers you to evolve into your mastery. You perceive that we are of some other echelon in the hierarchy of spiritual progression. We use the word humility to convey to you that you too have the same capacities. And you are coming into an understanding of this power, these capabilities, this ability while on the earth plane - while walking the earth. And we congratulate you for this.

Take a moment and fill yourself with the blessing that we offer to you now. What you have just done is availed yourself to light, and what we will discuss tonight is joy, and pleasure, and availing ones self to more light. You have been conditioned, or brainwashed, into believing that life must be a difficult, painful and arduous experience. You have believed that there would be many, many obstacles in this life. You have used that belief to create a life experience that is the reflection of the belief. So you have created many difficult obstacles in this life. The teachings that we offer you give you the insights and the power to eliminate this belief from your mind. The work that we do with your energy helps to facilitate the process of removing this belief from your energy fields and opening the aspects of your consciousness to a new belief with respect to having the ability and the capacity to retain joy.

We would first discuss the reason that joy is not pursued. We would say that in the Judeo-Christian culture, there is a strong undercurrent belief that joy is to be postponed for a hereafter as a reward for righteous living in this life. The reasons for this erroneous belief are too numerous to discuss here. What we would say is that the belief that a heaven and/or hell exists in a place outside of this human experience fuels that propensity to postpone joy.

What you have learned, as your consciousness has expanded, is that there is no heaven and hell outside of this human experience. The heaven or hell that is experienced by a human is the state that the human creates through their consciousness in this life experience. And therefore, there is no need to postpone joy. There is only a need to understand that joy can be created at any time as one's beliefs become aligned with the unconditional love of which we speak. So there is no need to wait for your reward in heaven. Your reward is waiting for you immediately, as you align your thoughts and beliefs with GOD's unconditional love.

When you experience joy, it is often accompanied by a feeling of guilt. This guilt is due to the belief that the experience of joy flies in the face of the Judeo-Christian tradition, and therefore, you have a reluctance to create this joy. And that is why we would eliminate this myth from your consciousness now. There are many pathways to joy. There are many experiences that would give you joy. Of course, the experiences that are most aligned with your soul's purpose, and the exploration and experience of the unconditional love of GOD, are the paramount pathways to this joy. For GOD is this joy. GOD is this bliss. And as you recognize yourself as a creation of

GOD, and as a part of the wholeness of GOD, you too recognize and experience this joy and this bliss.

We would now discuss a misunderstood pathway to joy, and that is the experience of human sexuality. We would begin this discussion by sharing with you a perspective on the humorous occurrences that you are now experiencing.

<there was an unusual and excessive amount of noise and other distractions in the space that evening, including a late start, many people arriving late, a commotion in the parking lot, and people wandering in off the street asking for directions>

You are experiencing the creation of barriers to this understanding. Subconsciously, you knew this was coming. Subconsciously the channel knew this was coming, and was so reluctant to work with this information, that the channel created, and continues to create, many distractions. This harkens back to what we discussed moments ago about the human's reluctance to experience joy. So with that understanding, and with the very humorous illustration of how one's subconscious conditioning creates situations, we will move forward.

Human sexuality is misunderstood, and comes with many erroneous connotations, many misperceptions, and many untruths. Sexuality, like any endeavor, is an opportunity for the human to see where the consciousness is aligned with unconditional love, and where the consciousness is not aligned with unconditional love. In human sexuality, the human is given the opportunity to view themselves without defenses, and to create an experience of bliss, and joy, that is not unlike the experience of bliss and joy that is experienced when union with the light of GOD is experienced. However, in the process of this creation, insecurities about one's humanness are often triggered. Your task is to come to a new understanding of sexuality as simply an opportunity to experience bliss and joy, and a vehicle (like any other vehicle) to examine where one is loving ones self (and another, or others) completely and unconditionally, and where one is not. This is actually quite simple. In "The Course in Miracles," there is a passage that indicates that nothing has meaning except the meaning that you give to it, because your consciousness creates it and gives it meaning. This is true of human sexuality. So we discuss human sexuality tonight to share with you the objective truth that it is simply an opportunity to experience the joy and bliss that is not unlike the joy and bliss of union with GOD, and to sustain it.

Human sexuality is also the opportunity to see where you are loving and accepting yourself and your partner, or partners, completely and unconditionally, and where you are not. Your experience of sexuality shows you where you have broken through the conditioning that you have received about this, and where you have not.

In the process of experiencing sexuality, the human experiences bliss, and joy, and peace, and comfort, and creativity. And are those not qualities of the light of GOD? In human sexuality, the human raises their vibration to the point where they are able to sustain more and more bliss and joy. Is that not the purpose of the pursuit of sexuality? Excuse us. Is that not the purpose of the pursuit of spirituality?

We offer humor because we want to draw a parallel. For sexuality and spirituality are not dichotomous, are not separated, are not opposites. They are one and the same in that sexuality is simply one way of many to explore one's spirituality. As you move forward with this understanding, it would be useful for you to invoke the love and light of GOD into your experience of sexuality. For that helps your experience of sexuality to fulfill its ultimate intent, which is more and more union, more and more enlightenment, a heightened vibration; for you invoke the fulfillment of this intent by bringing your sexuality out of the darkness and into the light. It is also useful for you to examine the many, many perceptions that you have about sexuality that are truly misperceptions.

So we will give you a moment at this time to go deeply within yourselves; and if you choose, write down any thoughts or beliefs that you have regarding sexuality.

Did anyone find any reactions to their views on sexuality that were surprising to them?

Group comment: This may be a topic we don't feel very comfortable speaking of in a group, which is why you are getting very little response from the crowd.

MASTERS: Yes. As we said before, there is a great deal of misperception, discomfort, and misunderstanding with respect to this topic. The conditioning about this runs deeply within the subconscious. That is why the environment seems unusually loud tonight, with many distractions. The collective consciousness is not comfortable, and is creating an environment of discomfort. Collectively you are creating distractions in order to not face the truth. The channel creates resistance as well. The channel subconsciously knew that this would be tonight's topic, and created many, many opportunities to delay this class.

We would move forward with this topic by saying that there is a great deal of judgment that has been attached to sexuality. Much of this judgment is condemning. Much of this judgment does not reflect the unconditional love of GOD.

Your task, as you move forward in a way that is comfortable for you, is to move past any conditions that you place on your ability to love yourselves, or your ability to love others, as reflections of the light of GOD that dwells within each of you. You may do this through prayer, you may do this through meditation, you may do this through a thorough inventory of your perceptions and beliefs, with respect to sexuality. By inventorying your perceptions and beliefs, asking yourself, "are those perceptions and beliefs aligned with GOD's unconditional love, or do they place judgments". Do these perceptions separate, do they demean, or do they deny a part of your wholeness?" What you are doing in this process is healing a large portion of your consciousness, and moving towards unconditional love. In addition, you are opening yourself to a higher level of creativity, and the ability to create that which you desire. For the creative power that is inherent in the experience of human sexuality becomes more open to you through the process of clearing your consciousness of these misperceptions.

So you may ask, "Why is this so important to spiritual growth and development?" And many of you are asking that question now. The reason that it is so important to spiritual growth and development is simply that it is part of the process of knowing yourself as your GOD-self -- your higher self. And using that knowledge of yourself to fulfill you divine intention -- your divine purpose. When you are not accepting a portion of yourself, or others, and when you are not owning and healing a portion of your consciousness to align it with the unconditional love and light, you are not growing spiritually. We strongly suspect that the reason you are sitting here is to grow spiritually. So when you examine your human consciousness, you certainly realize that much of it is based on the perception of sexuality - or more aptly, the misperceptions about sexuality. So as we move forward in facilitating the healing of your consciousness, we cannot help but to stumble over the misperceptions that form the lion's share of your consciousness.

Your discomfort with your sexuality is a natural human response, based on your human experience. What you are being asked to do is no small task. You are being asked to examine a part of your consciousness that is very deeply ingrained, and very deeply held, and is associated with much deep discomfort. And we will leave it at that. So we support you in your feelings of discomfort by sharing with you how natural they are, and give you the time you need to accept our healing light in a way and at a pace that you are able to accept it.

Question: What you have been discussing this evening, you have been discussing in a very non-emotional way and without any examples, which is not how you generally present information to us. Is there a way that you can give us an example on dealing with sexuality that is comfortable enough for the group to handle and understand?

MASTERS: Yes there is, and we will attempt to do so. We would first comment on a prior comment, which indicated also that the session this time was different from the session where sexuality was discussed in the previous class. Each time an event like this occurs, the energy from our realm is calibrated to work with the energy existing in the space at that time. There is a different cast of characters in this class than before, with resultant different energies. There is a different energy on the earth now than before. And there is a different energy in this physical space now than before. So the energy always comes through in a different way - in the way that is designed to be for the greatest good of all on many levels.

An example of the understanding of sexuality follows. Sexuality is an opportunity to experience and sustain joy and bliss. It is an opportunity, with your partner or partners, to explore the many ways that this can be experienced on a physical level. The purpose of the experience of this joy and bliss is to raise the vibration so that more light can be absorbed. Sexuality on the earth plane became distorted, and the perception of sexuality became defined by a very limited human consciousness that would control humans by closing off gateways to the higher self. The original intent of sexuality was a physical, spiritual ritual which would open the energy field to more and more light. This intent was purposefully lost as a consciousness that was not loving began to permeate the earth and to try to control others into believing that they did not have an individual connection with the light. So you see, sexuality as a pathway, or gateway, to the absorption of light was not consistent with the consciousness that became prevalent on the earth. The consciousness that became prevalent on earth would control humans by convincing humans that the only way to contact the light of GOD was through a mediating body - a mediating organization.

As a result, sexuality was then branded taboo, because in truth, it was an individual channel to the light and bliss of GOD. The dominant organization wanted to support the misperception that the only way to experience GOD was through the dominant organization. So the erroneous belief in the distastefulness, sinfulness, and harmfulness of sexuality became more and more the dominant consciousness for many on the earth. The inherent spirituality of sexuality was, for the most part, lost.

That is why it is physically uncomfortable to hear this. Some of you are experiencing physical discomfort, in addition to the mental and spatial discomfort, that you experience through the distractions. For we are working with a part of your consciousness that is deeply ingrained, and pervades many, many of your thoughts. And there is a reluctance to release that, and a difficulty releasing it, and this is why this session seems different.

In terms of physical examples, when engaging in the expression of sexuality in any way, you may choose to continually ask yourself, "How do I feel about this? What are my reactions to this?" As you are becoming more and more aware of your consciousness, you are starting to do this automatically in any situation. You are beginning to ask yourself, "How do I feel about this? What is my reaction to this? Why am I having this reaction?" With respect to the expression of your sexuality, what you may find is that you are bringing to your consciousness feelings of perhaps shame, inadequacy, fear of true expression, or fear of being seen "naked" in the literal and figurative sense of the word.

When you experience these feelings, they expose you to a part of yourself that is not aligned with unconditional love. So your task, if you choose to accept it, it to pray for realignment of your thoughts and your beliefs so that they may become aligned with unconditional love. Love yourself completely and unconditionally without judgment. Love your body completely and unconditionally without judgment. Know that GOD loves you completely and unconditionally without judgment. Feel GOD's loving presence in all ways, and as you experience your sexuality. This is how you invoke the light of GOD into your sexual expression. The experience of your sexuality need not be a furtive, dark act of shame or of desperation. It can be a beautiful exploration and expansion of bliss and joy, and merging of the light that is bliss and joy with your consciousness.

We would also draw a parallel for you. We would draw this parallel in the form of a question. Do you realize how many images of sexually you are bombarded with on any given day? If you ponder that question, then you realize how deeply ingrained sexuality is in you human consciousness. And when you realize how deeply ingrained sexuality is in your human consciousness, you realize then the importance of dealing with sexuality when one is trying to transform one's consciousness. For if one is trying to transform ones consciousness, one must pay attention to that which comprises some 80% of one's consciousness.

We will state affirmations, which you may repeat:

I love myself completely and unconditionally.

GOD loves me completely and unconditionally.

I love and accept every aspect of myself.

Every aspect of myself is of GOD.

I love and accept my sexuality.

Every aspect of my sexuality is of GOD.

I am innocent.

I am perfect.

In my innocence and in my perfection, I accept myself completely.

Good. Now we are making progress with your energies. In summary we would say, be not afraid of joy and pleasure. Understand that as you grow in the light, your experience of joy and pleasure will increase. And your ability to sustain joy and pleasure will increase. One aspect of this is the experience of your sexuality in a freer, more joyful, and more light-filled way. For this is a tool of your healing and your realignment with light.

Question: Celibacy has been, on this plane, thought of as one of the greatest sacrifices for the divine aspect. On your plane what is the thinking also of this.

MASTERS: That is a great sacrifice. We would begin our response to this in earnest by relating why celibacy is perceived as a sacrifice, and why it is exalted by some on the earth plane, or has been at certain times. For the sponsoring thought was that sexuality disconnected the human from GOD, and therefore the lack of sexuality through celibacy would connect the individual with GOD. We would also say that celibacy is a choice, and it has its purpose.

If a soul feels that it is not equipped to handle its sexuality, or if a soul truly, truly, truly believes that the only way that they can be aligned with GOD is through celibacy, then that will be their experience. For that is what they will create. However, many souls may not fully believe this. And therefore, celibacy may provide a conflict that is based on the tension between differing beliefs being housed in the same vessel of consciousness. We would not judge celibacy, as we would not judge any other expression, or lack of expression, of spirituality. They are all tools to be used to align with the light and truth of GOD.

You can gauge your alignment with the light and truth of GOD by gauging your experience of joy and bliss. Where you are experiencing joy and bliss, then you are more aligned with the light and truth of GOD. Where you are not experiencing joy and bliss, the lack of joy is the indication that there is disharmony between your consciousness and the truth of GOD. This disharmony causes discomfort, which draws your attention to this perception and gives the you an opportunity to heal the perception. Therefore, if celibacy does not offer you an opportunity for joy and bliss, but instead creates inner conflict, you must ask yourself if celibacy is for your greatest good. In that case, perhaps dealing with the conflicts caused by celibacy is for your greatest good because it leads you to a deeper healing.

Question: Does spirit view masturbation as unity with GOD?

MASTERS: GOD views all sexual expressions, where your experiences and explorations of sexuality and its creative potential open you to the joy and bliss of GOD as being aligned with the Love and Light of GOD. Again, we would say that the consciousness that has dominated the earth would separate you from your sexuality and its expression. We have given the reason that the dominant consciousness would do that, and that would be so that bodies, or institutions might insert themselves as intermediaries to the light of GOD, instead of empowering individuals to experience the light of GOD individually through their experiences of joy and bliss. The myth about masturbation that you allude to in your question is part of that dominant consciousness. So we would, through our response, clarify for you this myth.

Question: How does GOD view homosexuality?

MASTERS: With unconditional love.

Question: Spirit, will the dominant consciousness change?

MASTERS: Yes. And you are a catalyst for changing the dominant consciousness. And before you make your heart heavy by taking on a Messiah complex, we would say to you that you already are performing this task in a wonderful way. For as you raise your vibration and become a stronger and clearer vessel of light, the light from our realm of existence is able to manifest more and more on the earth. A chain reaction occurs as the light on the earth builds to a critical mass that changes the broad consciousness. This chain reaction continues and is facilitated by each and every one of you as you open to your light. This happens in obvious ways, such as the guidance and support that you give through what you teach others. And it happens in subtle ways as you increase your capacity to bear light. And this light is added to the repository of light on the earth that heals the earth and the earth's consciousness.

Question: How does the spiritual deal with child abusers or those who force themselves on others through sexuality.

MASTERS: First of all, abuse is not an act of sexuality, it is an act of physical, emotional and spiritual violence. In this case, the case that you describe, there is a teaching, a learning, and a healing occurring. This case (through an act that your human consciousness would judge as heinous, or hateful, or violent), the individuals who are involved see where their consciousness is aligned with light and love and where it is not. For when an act of violence or hatred is expressed, it is an expression of the individual's inner pain, turmoil and misalignment. The act and/or its consequences will give the individual an opportunity to examine the behavior and the consciousness behind the behavior to see where it is aligned with the light and where it is not. With respect to the party involved (that your human consciousness would term the innocent victim), this party (in the act that you describe) may have many purposes in agreeing to play a role in that drama.

We would begin by explaining the purpose that this "innocent victim" would have by saying that from the infinity of life, where the soul is housed, the human experience (and even the numerous human experiences that any individual expression of GOD's light has created), are a small portion of the soul's infinity. The vast majority of the soul's consciousness is housed in the realm of bliss, and comfort, and peace that does not know pain. So the small portion of the soul's consciousness that participates, views this experience as a small price to pay for a wonderful lesson that will be taught to the innocent victim, and to the perpetrator of the act of violence or hatred.

Question: It's really more than a fear, I have had very good reasons to believe that my three children have been abused. And

I need some explanation in how (if there is anything I can do) to help them. The eldest daughter is not 13, and she doesn't recall anything, but I've found some things in her room that she has definitely been exposed to some things we never exposed her to. One therapist thought that sometimes the children take on the role of the oppressor. The youngest one is not seeing anyone right now, she is only 4; at the time she was just a baby. I guess I need some guidance and help on how to help relate to my children what has happened. They don't have any recollections, at least right up in their memory. They can't recall anything. I think that they have stuffed it.

MASTERS: We will paraphrase your question to its basic elements. Your question is: "How may I support my children, and how may I help them to develop fully without fear and shame, so that they will be unfettered in their expansion and in their experience of life. You are receiving a deep healing and a deep light expansion from us now, which is also being sent to your children. Also, it will be transmitted directly through you as a result of this process. There are many others who are with you now in body (and of course in spirit) who are working with you and guiding you and others through this situation to lead it to the ultimate healing that will definitely occur from this situation. This situation for you has compelled you to love, protect, and support your daughters, and in a more unconditional way than you might have otherwise. This situation has compelled you to heal yourself and, therefore be a conduit of light and healing for your offspring as well. What you can consciously do to support them is more of what you are already doing. Expressing your love for them in every possible and conceivable way - explicitly and implicitly - continually reminding them of their innocence, and of their perfection, and of their GODliness in a way that is comfortable and natural for you. Invoking the light of GOD in your relationships with them so that the light heals them in a way that is effortless for you, and it will occur. Always, always, know that any situation that occurs is for the greatest good of all. Your offspring (through this experience) are understanding, and will continue to understand, love without condition and an outpouring of support that will strengthen and guide them throughout their lives. We would affirm that they will be firmly on their path. They will make the transition from childhood adulthood comfortably and peacefully through this process. By opening to the light of GOD, you will ensure that this transition from childhood to adulthood be made in a comfortable way by your offspring.

We would move into a discussion of karma. Because many of you have the question, "How does karma play into the experience of victimization in this life?" We would draw your consciousness to a passage from a book. The book is the book "Mutant Message from Down Under" by Marlo Morgan. In one chapter of this book one of the characters in the book fell and broke his leg. From a higher perspective, the purpose for the fall was that the character agreed (on the level of his higher self) to fall and break his leg in order to illustrate and teach. The experience was designed to teach the woman who was walking with these aboriginal peoples how healing can occur almost immediately when the energies are aligned with the powerful light of GOD. So the volunteer in this situation volunteered to fall and break his leg. Your human consciousness might judge this to be a very painful act. However, from the infinity of life where the soul was housed, that seemed like a small price to pay to teach a valuable lesson to many, many millions of people who subsequently read the book. The lesson that was taught was how the infinite power of GOD, when focused can manifest through humans and can heal a situation almost immediately with seemingly supernatural results.

We would give you another example. The example is the infant Bailey Alman, that appeared on the cover of several national magazines when your city Oklahoma was bombed. This souls (who you might term as an innocent victim) was actually a spiritual volunteer, who volunteered for this task in this short life to illustrate something in a very, very meaningful and visceral way, to literally millions of inhabitants on the earth. The being volunteered to illustrate the senselessness and destructiveness of hatred. To do so, this small child appeared on the cover of national and international magazines as the infant being held in the rescue workers arms, and appeared repeatedly in pictures throughout the world. From the limited perspective of the human consciousness, this child may have been viewed as an innocent victim. In truth, this child was a soul volunteer who taught a wonderful lesson to millions of people through a seemingly tragic event. The lesson this child taught was that hatred can have devastating effects, so humans should choose love at every juncture.

You may ask, "Was it this child's karma to be a victim?" That denotes, or judges, that this experience was somehow bad or tragic. Again, from the infinity of life, where the soul is seated, there are no bad, or good events. There are only events, and all events lead to GOD. All events are designed to show alignment, and to teach where the consciousness is aligned and where it is not, and to compel the consciousness to move towards alignment. For that is the soul's purpose. So was this event this person's karma? It was not because this soul had committed some heinous act in some prior life, and this soul was being punished. It was simply that this soul wanted to have this experience.

The reason that we bring up the law of karma, is because many of you associate "bad" (or what you would term "bad experiences") with karma. We would say that you are never destined to have any experience. Many of you associate "karma" with destiny and therefore feel that certain events are unavoidable. Karmic patterns are simply tendencies that would create the situations that a person needs in order to grow spiritually. However, the Law of Grace can enable you to grow without choosing painful experiences. The Law of Grace (which is the law of transformation) supersedes the law of karma. And what that means for you, is at any given time you can choose a new path, and you do not have to have experiences that your human consciousness would deem to be unfortunate. For if you come to a new awareness without having the experience, then why would you create the experience? This is another point that we wanted to make in this way. Does this begin to help you understand how an act of violence can ultimately be an act of love for you?

Question: I have a question. The information that you have shared with us over the last few sessions - it seems that we are drawing to us, or perhaps we are just recognizing it now, more situations that put us in a position to understanding these teachings that you are bringing to us. And I seem to be drawing to me, or people are being drawn to me, that bits and pieces of the conversations that we have had over the last few weeks would be beneficial to them. Is this something that we can share outside of this group?

MASTERS: Yes, you may share it as you are comfortable with it. For its purpose is to heal and to touch many.

CHAPTER 10.
THE DIVINE NATUF
OF PROSPERITY

Once again it with joy, and honor, and humility that we approach you tonight for you are all masters. You are masters because you have accepted the responsibility for this lifetime for your soul's growth and progression. You have availed yourself to the tools on earth, and the light of GOD that is within you, to help you in the process of bringing your infinite energy, power, wisdom to the forefront. We thank you for this. We thank you for the service that you are committing for the earth. With each step that you take in your own path of growth and development, you are adding more light to the reservoir of light that appears on the earth. You are doing your part to heal your consciousness, as well as the mass consciousness in ways that are difficult to describe, except by using the analogy of a contagious cold. So we thank you for this, and we honor you for this.

We would talk tonight in more detail about prosperity. If you recall from previous sessions, we talked about the power of prayer, and the ability of prayer to influence future probabilities, and to draw to you that which you desire. We talked about the invocation of prayer, as it sends more energy to the planning committee (in the creative realm), and it gives the planning committee more information to feed into their computer models, and then create the situation. So that is how prayer affects the outcome of the divine plan which brings to you what you desire. So we would not belabor the process of creation, there are other forums for that. You all understand the process of creative visualization. You all understand the process of envisioning and feeling as if you already have that which you desire. You already understand that GOD sees not lack. GOD only the infinite abundance that is GOD. And so we will not belabor that.

We would offer to you a prayer:

Mother/Father GOD, Creator, Sustainer, we open ourselves to the truth of our unlimited abundance. We open ourselves to the truth that nothing would be withheld from us. We open ourselves to the truth that your will is only that we be happy and fulfilled. For only when we are happy and fulfilled can we fulfill the divine plan for our lives, which is simply to magnify your light, your infinite creativity and your infinite love by exhibiting, exploring and experimenting with it. And therefore, reflecting and magnifying your essence. So we accept here and now our task, which is to open to this truth, and the reality of this truth in manifestation, which is our abundance. We release any guilt we might feel when we are creating while we see lack around us. We release guilt, and any misperception that we are undeserving. And we open to our heart's desires.

Question: I think it was last week that we talked about how I was dealing with symptoms, and not the root cause of things. And I guess I'm wondering, could you tell me specifically what the root causes are? I don't mind if everyone here knows of them. But the root causes of the situations I'm in regarding work, financial, which is the third time around on that one, and home.

MASTERS: We will answer your question in the best way for this forum, and in the best way that is for the greatest good for all. What we would suggest for you first, is that you build the scenario of your ideal life, your ideal home situation, your ideal work situation, and your ideal financial situation. Then you ask yourself "What prevents me from creating this?" You will find that as you write a list of those things that prevent you from creating this, you will find, at first, that they seem to be things outside your control. But as you examine those beliefs, you will instead find that they are beliefs that are in error, that are not aligned with the simple truth. And the simple truth is that GOD loves you completely and unconditionally. The simple truth is that you have permission to love yourself completely and unconditionally. And the root cause of what you perceive as difficulty is always a thought or belief that is out of alignment with the Simple Truth as we have outlined it.

We would not disempower you by outlining the many beliefs that you hold, which are inconsistent with the truth as we have outlined it. For that would actually impede your process. For it would rob you of the experience that you request, which is the experience of coming into awareness of yourself, not only at an intellectual level, but at a deeper level of your consciousness. If we were to outline in excruciating detail the beliefs that you hold deeply within your consciousness which are inconsistent with the simple truths which we have stated, we would keep them at a level that would be, how would we say, theoretical. These misperceptions would not be able to be recognized by you at a deeper level, and therefore be released to the Light of GOD. They would always be kept "at bay" on this mental shelf that you call your mind, in that part of your mind where you "will deal with things tomorrow." We love you.

Response: I know. Thank you. I love you too.

Question: May we have a prayer for greater alignment with the unconditional love of GOD?

MASTERS: With pleasure.

ᘓᘔᘓᘔᘓᘔᘓᘔ

Mother/Father GOD, Your unconditional light, Your unconditional love, Your deep, deep peace, Your innate harmony is the only reality I accept. Therefore, I align myself fully with Your light. I ask that Your light permeate me in a deeper way and bring me to balance, and bring me peace, and bring me power and bring me alignment with simple truth. The simple truth is that You love me completely and unconditionally. The simple truth is that the universe supports me completely and unconditionally, and that I have permission to love myself completely and unconditionally. And as I accept my task of self love, I align myself with Your love. For as I vibrate with unconditional love and acceptance for myself, I am in alignment with Your vibration. AMEN.

ᘓᘔᘓᘔᘓᘔᘓᘔ

Question: Yesterday I was offered the chance to rent a space in to do my healing. When I look at it, I can't make the decision because the space is not what I perfectly envision, but I know that I can't continue to do my healing work from my home. I'm confused and I can't make the decision.

MASTERS: You have called out to the universe for a gift of space. You then have created this space, yet there is a part of you from within that is not yet ready to accept it. Therefore, you do not see this space as a gift from the universe. The part of you that is not ready to accept this gift is the part of you that is in guilt and feels undeserving of this gift. The ego is also involved and has created a standard of perfection for this gift. The current gift does not appear to meet this standard of perfection. You are in conflict because a part of you also knows that you have created this space.

You may choose to accept this gift as part of your own loving self-acceptance. When you accept a gift of your creation, you send the universe the signal "I am worthy of this gift because I am loving myself and accepting myself more completely and as I love and accept myself more and more, I give myself everything that I desire. If you choose, then you can accept this gift. If not, you will create another opportunity to choose again, for opportunities are not static events. Opportunities continually re-create themselves as you continue to grow. No matter what choice you make, you are loved and accepted by the light of GOD, so you can love and accept yourself, and you can embrace every gift that the light of GOD would give to you.

This energy of self-rejection and rejecting the gift of GOD takes many forms and is very subtle, so we would offer you the following prayer:

Mother Father GOD, I open to the wisdom and the clarity to know, receive and accept every blessing, benefit and gift that you would give to me. I accept these gifts because I am lovable and acceptable just as I am and because you love me and accept me just as I am. Therefore, I accept your love, and your gifts just as I am. And so it is. AMEN.

There is also a pervasive belief that you must strive and strain and suffer in order to earn GOD's love. In truth there is nothing that you must do to earn GOD's love because GOD's love is so complete, so all-encompassing and fully available to you. GOD's love is available to you matter who you are, what you do , or what you think. GOD's love is available to you no matter who you were, what you did or what you thought. GOD's love for you is complete, unconditional and everlasting. Take a moment to accept and receive an energy of GOD's love here and now, in order to reinforce this truth.

You see, as you vibrate more in unconditional love and acceptance, you can draw to you more of GOD's unconditional love, which is the energy of light. As you accept more light, your energy field expands. As your energy field expands you are able to grow spiritually. As you grow spiritually, you are able to love and accept yourself more and more. As you love yourself more and more you are able to draw to you more of the energy of GOD, and this is an upward spiral.

CHAPTER 11.

EVERYDAY GUIDANCE – UNCONDITIONAL LOVING SELF-ACCEPTANCE

It is our honor and pleasure to work with you in this way. We would begin by suggesting that you prepare to receive a healing energy that would enable you to receive the information that we would offer.

You might repeat the following phrases:

I am open to healing my mind...

I am open to healing my energy...

I am open to healing my body...

In every way possible.

GOD's will for me is to heal every aspect of myself...

My will for me is to heal every aspect of myself...

I align my will with GOD's will and give the healing energy that comes to permission to move through me in a clear way.

That which I no longer need, I can discard...

I release any error in thoughts...

I release any misalignment of my energy...

I release any malfunctions within my body...

I release these things as my mind my body and my affairs are healed.

I open to receive the healing energy that comes to me now.

We would suggest that you focus on your heart chakra, feeling the heart chakra expanding with the light that comes to you now. Your heart chakra expands with the energy that comes to you now. Your heart chakra expands with the energy that comes to you now. An energy of tenderness, joy and embrace envelopes your heart chakra. Your heart chakra opens to an energy of love and peace and joy. Your heart chakra expands and expands and expands. You feel this expansion physically as it manifests in your physical body, and you feel your heart chakra expanding and expanding until the light of your heart chakra surrounds your whole physical body. you feel your heart chakra expanding and expanding until the light of your heart chakra surrounds your whole physical body. Your whole body is now wrapped in this wonderful bubble of light. Your whole body is now surrounded in this wonderful, loving warm cocoon of light. This bubble of light expands and expands. From the top of this bubble of light is a pillar of light that moves up through space, and it moves through the universe out to the creator. This pillar of light moves up from your bubble of light and connects you to your creator. You are so filled with light, and this pillar of light receives light from your creator. This light is moved into your personal bubble of light, and your bubble of light expands and expands. You now feel a strong and deep feeling of union with your creator. You now feel a strong and deep and lasting feeling of union with your creator. And you breathe, and you breathe, and you breathe, and you breathe. And all is well in your world.

We would then ask you to become aware of how you feel at this moment. We would ask if there is anything that would keep you from feeling the joy, bliss, peace and fulfillment. You may ask if there is anything that blocks you from these feelings. If there is anything that blocks you from your peace, joy, bliss and fulfillment, you may ask for it to be removed from you here and now.

In our discussion with you, we would begin talking with you about self-acceptance -- The importance of your self-acceptance on your Path to GOD. As an innocent and perfect soul that is and always been connected to the light of GOD, you understand your perfection, grace, power, beauty, and right to have joy. In that context you see yourself as part of a ray of light that shines from the heart of GOD (as opposed to an individual particle of light, disconnected from others).

However, as you have incarnated, you have believed the illusions that are apparent on the earth plane, -- the illusion of lack, the illusion of fear, the damaging effects of self-criticism, the damaging behavior patterns, the denigration of hatred and the challenges that face you on the earth plane. These things make you feel as if you are always in a struggle. They make you feel as if you never have what you need to succeed or survive. They make you feel less than divine. These qualities would send you a subtle message that you are disconnected from the light of

GOD, and therefore, unworthy of the Grace of GOD. When you receive these messages, you are not fully ready to accept your self, so you find it difficult to vibrate with the energy of unconditional loving acceptance – which is the essence of the energy of GOD.

Because you find it difficult to vibrate with this energy, you find it difficult to draw more of GOD's light to you, and you perpetuate self-destructive patterns. You perpetuate these patterns until you choose to see yourself and the world differently until you chose another consciousness that would enable you to accept yourself, vibrate with more unconditional Love, and thus draw more of GOD's Love and Light to you.

You are here where you learn to do this, because as you raise your vibration through prayer, meditation and emotional release, you begin to know yourself not by your human limitations but as the unlimited child of GOD. As you see yourself as the child of GOD, you evolve more, and vibrate with the Unconditional Loving Acceptance of GOD. You draw more of this Unconditional Loving Acceptance to you, and this becomes an upward spiral. This upward spiral embraces you, heals you and evolves you until you evolve in your GOD self. A key aspect of this process is self-acceptance, self-love, self-support, self-affirmation, and self-embrace.

Take a moment to take this in at a deeper level. Give yourself a chance for any nervousness, conflict or doubt to release from you in any way that it must.

In the past, you have believed that it is more important to love others than it is to love yourself. You have believed that it is important to martyr yourself by giving of yourself until there is nothing left to give. Your have believed that in order to atone for what you believe to be your shortcomings, that you must subjugate your needs in deference to the needs of others. These beliefs have not served you well, because these beliefs have not enabled you to evolve into the pure beings of light that you really are. These erroneous beliefs were based on the guilt. This guilt evolved from the misperception that you were somehow separate from the light of GOD, and that somehow you had strayed from GOD's grace. You then believed that you must atone and struggle in order to get back into GOD's good graces. In truth, you have never left GOD's good graces. You were created from the light of GOD to emanate from the Heart of GOD in order to expand GOD's consciousness. You are a part of the whole of GOD just like a small particle of light is just a part of a whole beam of light that emanates from a flashlight. As such, you need not reject yourself, denigrate yourself, withhold from yourself or in any other way cause yourself pain or suffering. It is important for you to release yourself from the conscious or subconscious desire create pain and suffering in your life.

Instead you must embrace yourself. You must know that you are lovable and that you deserve love. You must know that there is a well of love within you, and that this is your GOD Light. You must know that you are never judged, for GOD does not judge you, GOD only loves you. You must also know that you are never rejected by GOD or punished by GOD – GOD only embraces you. You are a part of GOD. GOD would not reject itself. GOD would not punish itself.

Your guilt would cause you to reject yourself or punish yourself. Therefore, we would suggest that you take a moment to take in an energy of self-love, self-embrace, self-acceptance, compassion for yourself, patience with yourself – no matter where you are in this life, and no matter what you have or have not done in this life. Take a moment to feel this new energy of - self-acceptance coming to you now. Take it in. Revel in this new energy of self-acceptance that you have not experienced before. Revel in it. Enjoy it. Good.....and breathe...

The New Truth is that GOD's love begins and ends with you. You have been taught that in order to gain love and be lovable you must give of yourself, prove yourself, and earn love. Instead, the New Truth is that as you open to receive love from your direct connection with GOD, you fill your heart, mind and energy field with the love of GOD, and you give of this Love. However, you do not have to do this from a place of insecurity in order to be lovable. Instead, you do this from a place of fullness, where your cup runneth over.

This is extremely important, because as you give from a place of fullness where your cup runneth over, you change the dynamic. You eliminate any expectation that some sort of payback will come to you for what you do. As a result you eliminate the source of disappointment and you eliminate codependent energies that create pain and suffering for you and others. Instead, you create a dynamic where you are continually feeding yourself more and more of the light of GOD and this light continually flows through you in greater measure. This light then automatically flows out from you to the people places and situations that need this light. When this light flows through you, you find that you are never depleted. You then find that you are never in fear or doubt and you never expect to be mistreated. Instead you find that you are always in a place of peace, because you are always being fed by the light of GOD. You are feeding others with your excess. The key here, again, is self-love and self-acceptance, because self-love is what draws more and more of the light of GOD to you. As you vibrate more and more with this energy, you learn to nurture yourself and cherish yourself and give to yourself more and more. Then you need not look outside of yourself for that which you need. You need not look outside of yourself for affirmation. It then becomes impossible for you to cause yourself pain and suffering.

Question: After Sunday's Service <which was extremely pivotal for the person>, it seemed as if I was getting sicker and sicker and sicker. There was a part of me that said, "I must be responsible and go to work" but there was another part of me that said "this is a chance to pamper myself". I surprised myself by being able to stay home and pamper myself without guilt. My question is, was my getting sick a result of the Sunday Service, or was it lesson in self-acceptance, or was it "D – all of the above".

MASTERS: As you know the answer was "D – All of the above". As you know, you had a major expansion in your energy as a result of Sunday's Service. You overcame several barriers that your ego, your fears and your memories of the past had placed in front of you. You grew spiritually, because these barriers were removed. The spiritual resources from within you that you called upon helped you to heal and overcome these barriers. However, drawing these resources to you required a substantial amount of energy, and when this process was complete, the light within you moved into even deeper places within you. You then became aware of deeper yet more subtle conflicts within you, and it seemed like you were in a new place (which in fact you were because you were vibrating on a new level).

As a result you needed to find a new equilibrium because there was much more light and it was as if you were navigating in a different atmosphere. You needed to learn to navigate in this new "spiritual atmosphere" in the same way that a human being would need to learn to navigate the moon's surface due to the difference in pressure, gravity, etc. In summary, your vibration changed and your energy changed, and the light moved into a deeper level of your consciousness, uncovering deeper levels of conflict. As a result, you needed rest, and you needed to regroup, and you needed to get acclimated to the new level of energy coming to you and to get acclimated to your new vibration. As a result you decided (on the level of your higher self) to get sick in order to rest and get acclimated to the changes.

Through this drama, you demonstrated the lesson that we just discussed, which is that the most important thing you can do in serving others was for you to love yourself, honor yourself, nurture yourself and pamper yourself. You "vessel of light" was somewhat depleted, and you know that in order to serve others you must give from overflow, which means that at times you must replenish your own "vessel of light". As you know, as "vessels of light" whose job it is to water the plants on the earth plane (the other beings on the earth plane), you cannot be effective in watering the other plants if your pitcher is depleted. When your pitcher of light is depleted, you must return to the source to replenish it.

This is an illustration of the importance of self-acceptance and self-love, because otherwise, your ego would have said "in order to be lovable, I must give and give of myself until there is nothing left". Instead, you said, I must give to myself so that I can give to others from my surplus.

Question: There was an incident in the news recently about a woman who was beaten up while she was jogging. Although I have been feeling more loved recently, I have also been feeling more fear as a result of this incident. I am wondering –is there a lesson in this.

MASTERS: The process of enlightenment is a very complex and iterative process. As you reach enlightenment, you are filled with more light and you feel more loved and embraced. However, your energy field has many layers in the same way that a tree has many rings when you look at its trunk. Your energy field consists of all the experiences on the earth plane from your current and prior lives. As a result, you carry the imprints of eons of experience on the earth plane. Most of the imprints that you carry reflect the energy of fear and guilt because these have been the predominant energies on the earth plane. So within your energy field are layers of fear based energies.

When you receive major light, this light moves in and heals you. However, this light is always penetrating deeper and deeper layers of your energy field and making you aware of deeper levels of fear and guilt that you hold. So it may feel like you have taken two steps forward and one step back in your growth. However, in truth, the light that has been expanded within you has simply touched a deeper place and it seems that you contract.

However, you do not contract to your prior level, because as you heal, you draw even more light to you so that you heal even more. You are constantly moving forward, healing, transforming and evolving your soul. Do not doubt that you have made progress. Do not doubt that you will make even more progress. This occurrence is simply the outer world's way of showing you the fear that you have contacted from within, because when you submit this fear to the light of GOD for healing and transformation, a deeper part of you is healed and then vibrates in unconditional love.

We would then suggest the following prayer:

Mother Father GOD, Great Spirit, our Creator. I open myself to receive your light. I open myself to receive your love. This light and this love heals me of my fears here and now. This light and this love fills me with a blessed assurance that I am embraced, protected, safe and free. With this truth, I open to receive more joy, bliss, comfort and peace. And so it is. AMEN.

Question: Yesterday I was feeling blissful. Today I felt such a deep anger. How can my mood swing so drastically from day to day. Can you give me some clarity on this? I think it has to do with feeling invalidated by everyone and needing to scream to get attention. I screamed at the repair people to the point where I am embarrassed. I think that those feelings of anger and my embarrassment go back to my own lack of self-acceptance, which you have discussed. Can you give me some clarity on this?

MASTERS: From the perspective of energy, you had a major expansion, and this expansion of light within your energy field touched a part of your consciousness where you were not yet ready to accept yourself because you felt invalid. This triggered an experience in your outer world where did not feel validated. This experience was designed to show you a part of your consciousness that was in need of additional healing. As a result, you reacted in anger because you did not feel affirmed. This new awareness then caused you to open to more light and healing, so it served its divine purpose. Forgive yourself, yet in truth there is nothing to forgive because this event was designed by you for your further growth, and thus is a wonderfully divine event.

You see, this process is an iterative process of growth and contraction. To accept this process and the many steps that it may take, you must also understand that there may be times when if feels as if you are taking two steps forward and one step back. There may be times that you feel that you may be "backsliding" but accept yourself even then. Know that you are of loving intent at all times. Know also that you are always forgiven, yet there is nothing to forgive.

The continuing challenge in this life is to learn to live without guilt and instead to live with unconditional loving acceptance for yourself. Unconditional loving acceptance is the antithesis of guilt. You are given many opportunities to heal the parts of you that feel that it must contain guilt and therefore would reject itself or withhold from itself out of a feeling of guilt.

Question: Was there a lesson for the repair people involved in this? Did they get something out of this for their growth, too?

MASTERS: Yes. They learned that they need to listen. <laughter>

Question: Along those same lines, and in light of the lesson of self-acceptance, it is not a perfect world so as we go along there may be some damage done in the learning process. I am at a crossroads where there is a lot of chaos. Sometimes I really need an answer NOW. I need to know how to get that answer immediately and accurately in the midst of chaos.

MASTERS: This is a very complex question. It has implications for all. Therefore, we will answer it in a way that has meaning for all, yet protects your privacy. For those who listen to this question, there is a need to understand the divine nature of chaos. You are in a very creative part of your existence on the earth plane where you are creating for yourself and others a new level of existence. You are moving to a new spiritual level. In this divine chaos, everything conceivable seems to be thrown "up in the air" because all the pieces are being re-formed in a new way. It is much like the "building analogy" -- for a new building to be erected, the old building may have to be imploded so this may seem like a chaotic process. Yet this is all part of a divine process.

During any period of this divine chaos, it is important that you trust the process of growth, healing and re-formation. As this relates to your current situation and your need for quick succinct direct and accurate answers, we recommend that you retreat back to your center. At your center, you can quietly, peacefully and deliberately contact the highest guidance available to you. You can tap into this energy by continually practicing prayer and meditation to expand and fine-tune your channel during times when you are not experiencing chaos. By tapping in regularly when you are not in chaos, you develop a "track record of trust" that enables you to tap into the "well of light" easily even during chaotic times.

The next thing that you might choose to do is to create a methodology to tap in immediately no matter what the situation. We would offer you an example. The channel will touch his belt buckle often when giving a spiritual message. The channel does this because he has conditioned himself to associate touching his belt buckle with tapping into the highest realm of consciousness available to him in any situation. The channel has conditioned himself to do this by "tapping in" while touching his belt buckle on numerous occasions. As a result, the association between the channel touching his belt buckle and "tapping in" became stronger and stronger. Just as Pavlov's dog associated food with hearing a bell ring, the channel associates touching his belt buckle with "tapping in", and then immediately opens to receive the highest guidance available. You might consider developing a similar association. If touching your belt buckle is infeasible, another method such as touching your thumb and your forefinger together might be equally effective. You might also consider touching your eyebrow, pulling up you sock, or adjusting your panty hose (in a socially appropriate way).

Question: I have been seeking the universe for a living space as well as a space for practicing the healing arts, do you have any guidance on this?

MASTERS: It is very helpful for you to write down what you want again and again. Refine your desire. The living space appears to manifest in the next 2 to 3 weeks. It is very important for you to add more creative energy to this without any anxiety. So if you write down what you want , you might consider doing so while in a meditative state. By expressing your desires in a meditative state, you can more easily release any anxiety that would otherwise thwart your creative process. You see, any energy of anxiety is inconsistent with the unconditional love of GOD, because anxiety says "GOD would withhold from me, I do not have enough, and I am afraid". These energies of lack and fear repel the energy of unconditional love, and instead invite their reflection (more lack and fear). So while you are in your prayerful space, you may bring up any anxieties and fears and release them to the light. Then from a place of peace, you can write, visualize and create your heart's desires.

Question: I've received the most spectacular gifts from spirit – my reward for a lot of work that I have done on myself. In the midst of it, a good friend is offended by something that I either said or did. I am not sure what to do about it now, and my inner sense tells me to be silent for a while. Do you have any guidance on this.

MASTERS: What is occurring here is that your vibration has shifted or changed. This individual senses this shift on several levels and your energies are not compatible at this moment. This individual is not comfortable with this change because this individual would rather have you back where you were, for that is where the individual was comfortable with you. This situation was created as a trigger to help you both see the disparity between where the two of you are. Do not judge this disparity. Understand that this is part of the iterative process of growth. This will take time to work out.

In the meantime, you can work in your own energy of prayer and meditation to communicate with this individual's higher self. You can do this by going into your space of prayer and meditation and communicating all the things that you would normally say in person to the individual. You will be communicating with this person's "higher se time, the individual is not ready to hear what y a human level. If you communicate subjective we suggest, you let the individual know what i why you did what you did, and apologize, these go for in helping this relationship to come back into balance. You might also ask to see the truth in this situation for yourself. The truth is that there is a degree of envy here – a subtle jealousy here. The healing that you send to this individual will help to rebalance this to some degree.

Question: Recently I've been feeling a void in my life that I have never felt before. How can I get rid of this void without causing havoc in my life?

MASTERS: You have been doing work with yourself on many levels. Some of these levels are know to you, and some are unknown to you. There are times when you have a "major clearing". A "major clearing" is a major shift in your perception and a quantum leap where old patterns, thoughts and habits and some spiritual guides are no longer a part of your life. There is a time before the new energy, the new patterning and the new spiritual guides settle in. This is the period of the void. Certain of your spiritual guides may have been there for a specific purpose, which has now been fulfilled, so they move on to make room for new guides and teachers. During the period of the void, you can make yourself available for more prayer and meditation so that you may connect more deeply with the light of GOD. You can then ask "what are the next steps that I may take to create the next stages of my hearts desires". You will then be guided to the stimuli that will move into the void and move you along to creating your next level of bliss. When you are in the void, you can take time to rest in GOD because you do not have to always struggle.

Take a moment to take in the thought *"I do not always have to struggle always. I can rest in GOD. I can rest in the blessed assurance that there is a time for action and there is a time for inaction. There is a time for the creative male energy, and there is a time for the passive female energy that is receptive,*

death so that his energy and essence could after death re-contact the individuals with whom he was close, this being was able to prove the eternal nature of the soul. And this being did this so that humanity could have a new perspective on life and living, and <so that humanity could have> a new way to see life. Do you understand? The purpose of this act was to heal and transform erroneous thought processes such as "this life is all there is" and other erroneous thought processes– so many thought processes that we cannot begin to catalogue them due to the constraints of time and the energy in this forum. The point of this was that this being volunteered to do this in order to eradicate erroneous thinking. Sin is simply erroneous thinking. So the phrase "Christ died for your sins" actually means that this being --who always knew of his divinity while on the earth plane (and embodied many aspects of divinity while being encased in a human body) – this being volunteered to have this "death" and "resurrection" to prove the eternal nature of the soul so that humans could think more clearly and understand their eternal nature. That is what the essence of the phrase "Christ died for your sins" means.

There are those on the earth plane who use this phrase frequently, but if pressed to explain what it means, would be "hard pressed" to do so. Do you understand? <yes> We would then continue with this. The essence of the teachings of Jesus the Christed Man was love. Love of neighbor as self, --of wisdom, faith and love, the greatest of these is love, -- seek ye first the Kingdom of Heaven from within (which is love) and all else shall follow, -- love reneweth all things, -- this was the essence of the teachings of this being. Do you understand? <yes>

There have been many who have put words in this being's mouth posthumously. Do you understand? <yes>

What you must know is that the sole purpose of the being that you identify as Jesus is to help you to heal, to transform, to overcome your limited vision based on your humanity and your limited sight based on your humanity so that you know yourself also as Christed beings so that you too may transcend your physical limitations and the limitations of the earth plane and manifest all the characteristics of your creator and the Kingdom of Heaven while on the earth plane.

Your task is to merge your eternal soul energy (which is and always has been connected with the heart of GOD) with your human energy in such strong measure that your Christedness subsumes your humanity. That is how you create and sustain the Kingdom of Heaven here on earth. Do not for a moment think that you are unworthy or ineligible for the Christed energy, for as you open and receive and heal and give the energies of light permission to transform you, you too are Christed. As you relinquish any power that you believe that the earth plane has over you, you too transcend. As you give yourself permission to love yourself and to be loved so completely and unconditionally that your energy field vibrates at such a high rate that you are compatible with so much of the energy of the heart of GOD, you too are Christed, while on the earth plane.

As you know, I have said "the things that I have done, you will do much greater things". This, at one time, was a prophesy. Due to the energy and healing that has taken place on the planet, this is now becoming a truth. There is no mystery to me. All you must do is call on me. You believe, on some level, that you are unworthy of receiving me. You are my Brother. You are my Sister. You and I are one. You are worthy simply because you are. There is nothing that you need to do to become worthy. There is nothing that you need to say to become worthy. You are worthy for you and I are one. Take a moment to receive a healing energy now, and let it move through you and let it move through you in whatever way that it would.

Be Blessed and in GOD.

Question: When I am trying meditation I sometimes feel I'm forcing myself to do something. I tend to get scattered, or not focused, and my mind tends to wander around on other things. A sort of attention problem, I guess, when I am trying to focus or send love to individuals. Its a llot easier with people I love, but even then, I tend to lose my focus sometimes. I wonder if you have any suggestions.

MASTERS: Yes. We would suggest that prior to going into a meditation session, that you do some writing or some visualization first. This process would force out of your mind the random thoughts that would otherwise invade your mind and threaten your concentration. If there is someone who has been on your mind, you may choose to either acknowledge them and have an imaginary conversation with them prior to your meditation so the thought of them does not randomly enter your mind. If there is a problem to be solved, or an event or occurrence to be resolved, you can see that event happening prior to your session. Or you can make a note of it prior to your meditation and forcibly think about it so that the random thoughts do not invade your mind. What you may also do is concentrate on an image, such as a candle burning, or some other image that seems to be stable. Force your mind to focus on it. Every time your mind wanders, force your mind back to that focus. Little by little you will discipline yourself to stay focused on the issue at hand.

Now with respect to the question about forcing yourself to do something that you may not feel that you are ready to do, we would give you two pieces of information and/or advice. We would say first of all, that all you have to do is have the intent. And we who will work with your energy will do the rest. If your intent is not to focus your heart energy on any individual at a given time, you always have free will not to do so at that time.

There may be other needs that you have, or that others have. These other needs may require your attention. Understand that the divine purpose is for you to always do only that which is in your free will.

We would say that your heart energy is opening quite wonderfully of its own volition. And your overall energy continues to open as it has opened over the last several years. As you have made yourself more available to the information that would help you to grow, you do not ever have to force your heart to open more and more, for it is already opening in a wonderful way. You must understand that the rhythm of the light which touches the earth, touches the earth with different velocities and different qualities at different times. There may be times when it is simply not in your greatest good to channel light from your heart in a heart meditation, for you may need the light for your own healing. There may be other things occurring within your energy field, or within the energy field of others, that would cause you not to be comfortable at that moment with heart meditation. You do not have to feel guilty about this. Simply understand that you are working in accordance with a divine plan. Trust this divine plan.

Question: I understand that humans choose the incarnation they wish to come into. They choose the life that they incarnate. Do animals also do the same? Do animals choose the species that they go to, or the particular family that they'll end up with?

MASTERS: Yes. It is all part of the divine plan.

Question: There was a time, not very long ago, when I felt very invincible, as if I was walking in my own energy and in my own power. And I had a very strong sense of self. However lately I have not been feeling that way, although I have been affirming the truth of who I am. And I need a clarification as to what is going on with me.

MASTERS: We would discuss with you the nature of expansion, because this is a natural phenomenon. As expansion occurs you draw in more light. This light touches a deeper level within you. Older, more deeply buried non-moving energies exist at this deeper level. These energies are not aligned with love, so when the light touches these energies, it feels as if your energy contracts. In truth, the light that you have drawn to you is concentrating on these energies to transform them and bring them into alignment. As a result, you draw in more light, and you expand even further. Then it feels as if you contract, for you are charting new ground in terms of deeper issues. So you do contract, but not to the level where you were before. You are constantly growing.

So the process of growth is dynamic, with expansions and contractions, and expansions and seeming contractions, and expansions and seeming contractions. When you are in a contracting period, you are impelled to draw even more light so you expand even more. That is why it may seem that you are taking two steps forward and one step back. What you need to understand about this process is that you are being walked through it by the energy that emanates from the heart of GOD. You are being guided in a wonderful and a very, very exacting way. You are being supported by many of us here who touch with you. When you feel doubt (and it may feel as if you are disconnected), your task is to affirm that connection through prayer and meditation as much as possible, for this will bring you back to alignment. Understand that the process of expansion and contraction, and more expansion and more seeming contraction is natural.

Question: Sometimes when there is fear, we feel it's gone after we've done emotional release. And later on, at other times it feels like it has crept back in some dimension. Maybe not to the same extent as before the attempted release, but there is a residual, or a backlash.

MASTERS: We would acknowledge this by first acknowledging the excellence and thoroughness of the process that you are using, and that you have used to release. You are doing wonderfully in your efforts and your endeavors. And you're opening to a magnificent amount of light. But we would say to you that you are not opening to anything new. You are simply opening to the magnificence of light that has always been you. You are just now recognizing the extent of this light, the depth of this light, the beauty of this light, and the magnificence of this light. You are removing from your eyes the shades and clouds of darkness that in the past colored, or dampened your perception of the light that you are. So we would acknowledge the wonderful work that you are doing.

What you must understand is two fold. That this is an iterative process, and that as you release a layer of fear, or guilt, or anger, or shame, or anything else, there may be a deeper level that lies beneath that level. As the light shines more deeply within you, and transforms every part of you, you sequentially will come across other levels of the same, or similar, area of work. But you become more comfortable with the process. You must understand that you are releasing aeons and aeons of negation, difficulty, suffering, pain, and subconscious memories that manifest now in fear. So you are moving through a seemingly infinite array of these energies from the infinity of your soul. But there is much help for this, and you will move through it wonderfully. There is much light to support you. When you release, the false-ego, which we have discussed in the past, is very creative. The false-ego is very disingenuous in wanting to remain a dominant part of your consciousness. It would point out additional areas, and taunt you in a way that would convince you not to do the work. For it would seem that the work is endless. And this is part of the false-ego's very clever drive to survive. For there are parts of the false-ego that fear it would be destroyed, when in fact it would simply and only be transformed, but it does not realize this yet. So you must understand that this is a very clever ploy of the false-ego.

Now we would not demonize the false-ego, for it is doing what it knows how to do as any organism would what it needs to do to ensure its survival. We would say that you must safely recognize objectively that this is a part of its operation. In recognizing that this is a part of its operation, you are prepared to teach it how not to operate in this way. You are teaching it how to accede to the process of enlightenment in a wonderfully cooperative way.

We would comment on the overall level of growth that has occurred within you all over the past week, and months, and years. You have all come a very long way in the evolution of your consciousness. And we support, applaud and shower you with light, or bless you, in what you have accomplished. We bring to you blessings and praise from the heart of our Creator for your participation, and your active and aggressive submission to this process of transformation to the light.

Question: First of all, I'm very grateful, appreciative and happy for all the blessings and miracles I've been receiving since I've started this class. Also I would like to affirm that I will continue to replace chronic struggle patterns. I would like to replace that pattern with more of a flow of confidence, and joy, and fun, and in pursuing my ability to spread my light to help people, and to have that be a fun process.

MASTERS: Yes. Would anyone else like to express their desire?

Question: I think I like the way that you put that chronic hardship problem. First of all, I am really thankful. This has been just a wonderful week. And I guess I'm always provided for. I mean, horrible things keep happening, but I know that deep down I am always safe. None of my worst fears have ever come true. Whatever you want to send, I am ready to receive it! And I would like it to come fast! I will just leave it at that. Do you know what I mean?

MASTERS: We would comment on your comment. We, at this time, simply send you love, and light and clarity in your thought processes. You will find in your mind that you will have a stronger ability to simply move to the root of any issue that causes you difficulty. In the past, many times you have focused on the symptom, and used your energy to address the symptoms. Now, through the process of evolution that you choose, you are moving to the root causes of those things which cause you difficulty. And once you eliminate the root cause, there is no longer any need to create the symptom that would make you aware of the root cause. For the root cause is then eliminated, eradicated and transformed by our light. So you have taken wonderful steps in this direction.

We would talk briefly about the consciousness of suffering. A deeply held belief in the overall human consciousness is that in order to grow spiritually you must suffer. This belief says that in order to show your true faith, one must have the patience of Job in the face of horrible adversity. We would say to you that the story of Job was simply a story. We would say to you that a belief that there must be suffering, and that divinity must be earned through suffering is an illusion. Your divinity is free. Your divinity is inherent within you. For your divinity **is** you. And you no longer have to earn what you already own. **You no longer have to earn what you already own.** Please make a note of this phrase.

We suggest that you repeat this prayer in unison to magnify the energy with which it is sent to our realm:

Mother/Father GOD, Creator, Sustainer, Lover of all Life, Lover of all Creation, Creator of all Life, Creator of all Creation, We release any perception that joy must be accompanied by suffering. We release any desire to learn the life lesson of unconditional love through pain and suffering. We open to a new way of living. We open to a new way of believing. We believe that all that we desire is given to us. We believe that nothing is withheld from us. We believe that you love us completely and unconditionally. Therefore, we believe that you would not punish us. Therefore, we believe that you would not make us suffer. We believe that your will for us is to be happy and fulfilled. We believe that your will for us is for

us to have everything, and for us to do everything, and for us to be everything that we desire. For this is truth. For in this truth we truly are your reflection, your infinity, your power, your grace, your creativity. We cast this prayer on the ocean of light that is your infinity. We give the ocean of light that is your infinity the permission to wash over us and heal our minds, so that we no longer believe that we must create pain and suffering in order to grow. We do not have to earn what we already own. AMEN.

~~~~~~~~

Question: I 'm feeling pretty scattered lately, and it would be really nice to have some focus, and a sense of direction, and some clarity. And I feel that the guidance I'm getting from spirit right now has to do with emotional healing, which I need, but it doesn't seem very focused on the outer world. And it's making me a little nervous to live with so much uncertainty. Can you address this?

MASTERS: Yes we can. You must understand that you outer world is created by your inner consciousness. And that by working with you inner consciousness and transforming it, you're investing in creating an outer world that is more affirming to you, and that gives you and reinforces for you the joy that you find within your heart.

On a practical level, the inner work, and the inner focus that you are investing in now will pay wonderful dividends to you in the not so distant future. You will know, and you have begun to know, of GOD's providence for you. You know that you are sustained by a light and a power that you have opened to. So we would confirm and affirm that your focus inward at this time is the focus that is for your greatest good. Now we
~~~~~~~~

would also suggest that you look at the litany of activities and options that you face right now in terms of how you spend your time, and your professional and spiritual endeavors which are beginning to emerge in a very interesting way for you. And we ask, if you choose, that you prioritize them in terms of your heart index. The heart index is the measurement that you take with the barometer of your heart that would tell you how aligned each activity is with your highest good. When an activity feels wonderful in your heart, and feels beautifully and powerfully affirming in your heart, then it has a high score on the heart index. When it feels less so, it has a lower score on the heart index.

Question: I've learned from another master, another spirit, through a different channel that there are many angels here on the earth plane now. Many, many angels. Those angels, do they know they are angels?

MASTERS: It depends on the divine purpose of the entity that is embodied.

Question: Have you incarnated in human form?

MASTERS: We would explain who we are more fully. We are a collective consciousness. We contain who have been individualized at one time or another, and some who have not chosen this plane of existence for their experience. We are a collective. We operate as a collective. For you see, as energy moves higher in its vibration, and closer in its path of reunification with The All, it collects.

Question: So parts of you have, and parts of you haven't.

MASTERS: Some have, some haven't.

Question: I have a question that is not too esoteric. I've always thought that my cats were angels. They're just so perfect. They're just always there when you need them. Can you address my pets, and anybody else's, and what role they play with Spirit?

MASTERS: You have created tools to continuously remind you of the truth. These are individualized consciousness that you brought with you, and that you created to remind you of unconditional love, of complete acceptance, and of the light in its innocent and perfect state. These are tools. This is very difficult to explain in a way that has meaning. This is difficult to express in the terms and perceptions of limitation. You see, in a sense, *you are all angels*. The human mind would stratify, and place in hierarchies, and separate things; but as the consciousness evolves, and should we say expands in light to the point where it is very similar to the source, those divisions are no longer because there is no separation. So the term "angel" is one that we have difficulty working with. For it is an invention, or a convention, of the perspective that is limited, and would need to categorize, and place in hierarchy.

Question: I would like to ask to get to know you better, because I've been working a lot with release this week. I've been doing a lot of crying, a lot of opening, a lot of releasing, and I just feel like I would like a little more joy, a little more love, a little more.....to replace some of this stuff that I've been able to get out. This is a very, very trying time for me. Because this is the week coming up to Mother's Day. And I was very close to my mother. And I have been trying to release a lot of stuff, a lot of tears, a lot of emotions, a lot of fears, things that I've been going through. So I'm asking for your help, and more love and more joy and more laughter.

MASTERS: Yes. You have found a new family – a family of Light. This Light, these beings, from our realm and beings that you also are in contact with on your realm, converge to fill a space that has been left by the physical absence of your mother. Your mother has not gone far. For she is with us now. And if you feel your left shoulder, you will feel her now.

The space that has been left is also being filled by the light and love of GOD. You are acknowledging this loss. And this is important, and you have our love, our support, in this process. Your loss is real. And know that your mother gives you a wonderful gift. For the light, and love, and space that her energy occupied in your heart is not empty. It is filled with the light and love of GOD that mixes with the light and love that is your mother. And we purposefully use the present tense, the light and love that **is** your mother. You may call on this light as you choose.

What is drawn to you as you call on this light is a wonderful ray that emanates from the heart of GOD, that feels comfortable, peaceful and joyful to you. It is a ray of light from the heart of GOD that feels familiar to you. For it is familiar to you. It is the energy that is the essence of your mother. Yet it is more powerful, more strong, more loving and more complete than it could ever have been while in the limited space of the earth. Do take comfort in this truth. Do take comfort in our love for you. Do take comfort in the reality of the infinity of life. We send you a healing energy now in support for you.

Question: Would you address the topic of addictions with this group? I need help in breaking some addictions that I have.

MASTERS: Yes, we would address that topic. Addiction is where the human perceives that some outside force would give them what they need to survive. For you see, when one has an addiction, one has a fear that if they did not have that thing to which they are addicted, they would not be able to survive. And that thing that they feel that they need to survive is what feeds them light, or so they believe. And so they imbibe, or ingest, or act out in pursuit of what they perceive as the life force in this thing that is outside of them as opposed to moving into alignment with GOD, and understanding GOD is that source. For example, an addiction to food, or anything, is a **substitution**.

Food may give the individual the feeling of being fulfilled and the feeling of being nurtured. When an infant is fed, it knows that it is getting what it needs to survive. And it learns to crave being fed. For at that time, it knows undoubtedly that it is receiving that which it needs for its life force. So it has substituted getting fed for the life source that truly comes from GOD, but comes through the conduit of another human being.

Well, an addiction is like that. An addiction substitutes

the need for sustenance from the Light of GOD with a need for something else such as food, drugs or sex. But another activity, or pursuit, is substituted. The temporary high that results from the addiction (such as sex, gambling, food or drugs) is a substitute for the bliss that comes through union with the light. We would say, judge not any addiction. Understand only that any addiction is a tool that has been chosen by the soul to compel it to align with the light. For any substitution that the human chooses is the tool of that human's choice to help them understand that substitution does not really work. Addiction only leads to pain and suffering that eventually compels the individual to open to GOD.

What can be done about addictions? Understand that the addiction is a part of the Divine Order that would ultimately teach the individual of its alignment with GOD through the individual experiencing the effects of nonalignment to the point where the individual no longer desires to experience those deleterious effects. So what we would say is little by little, release any pain. And pray for the release of any pain that others may have that causes them to substitute an activity, or a substance, for the direct ingestion of GOD's Light through prayer and meditation. That is how healing can occur in this situation. That is how the substitution of the secondary activity, or substance, can be removed so that the primary source can be connected with. Continual prayer relieves the pain and the lack that may cause, or lead to addiction.

Now what must also be understood about this is that prior to incarnation, the soul knows bliss, and only bliss, and only comfort, and only union. As a result, the soul may underestimate the human experience because prior to incarnation, the human experience is seen through the haze of bliss. Then the soul descends into matter by slowing down the vibration again and manifesting into a physical body (that is why we call it a descent from the expanded realm of light to the contracted realm of matter that is the earth plane). The soul has underestimated the human experience because it has been seen through the haze of bliss. Some humans have more difficulty with this, hence the prevalence of addictions.

There is a correlation between the community in which the individuals chooses to incarnate and the pervasiveness of addictions because of this occurrence. What we are saying is that in certain communities, such as perhaps disadvantaged or minority communities, the rate of addiction may seem to be higher. Prior to incarnation, the souls underestimated the difficulty of the assignment on the earth plane. And once on the earth plane, did not have all the tools necessary to navigate without the tool of addiction as a divine tool for realignment. We would also say that in time, with patience, with love, the substitution of truth occurs.

Regardless of the activity, or substance, or relationship that has been used by the individual to attain that feeling of fullness. Know and have compassion for all who choose these tools. For all are tools of realignment. Do not judge them or yourself. It this understood? For just as each human had different experiences, and a different vibration and velocity of light, each human has different tools that it takes on its journey back to the heart of GOD. Do not judge any tool that is used, for all are wonderful tools.

Question: My question is about this reoccurring that I am going through with my finances. And it's not even just that. I just feel like life is so crazy in all these little different things. And I am always running. And I'm in a very difficult time. I try to affirm that, "oh, this is going to be fine," and it actually really is when I stop to think about it. Because we haven't starved to death, and none of my worst fears have ever come true. I really want to let go of the fear. I don't know if I'm really explaining my question very well. I just need a break. Can you give me any insight on this, on maybe how to deal with this a little better?

MASTERS: As we read your energy, the predominant issue with you with respect to the things in your life that don't seem to go as smoothly as you would like, is that you have an unexpressed anger at GOD. In a very analogous way to the situation we described where at the level of the soul, prior to incarnation, you underestimated the difficulty that you might have navigating on the earth plane. Through this navigation you now feel, subconsciously, that you have been placed here, and abandoned here, by GOD. Subconsciously, you feel that if GOD truly loved you, GOD would not have placed you here in such a dense and inhospitable climate, and would not have left you alone. For the image that the channel is receiving is someone wandering on the desert.

So you have this anger, which goes unexpressed in many ways because it is anger at GOD. Part of your consciousness says that, "I cannot be angry at GOD, for GOD is Divine and will punish me if I express anger." Your task is to let yourself be an angry child at GOD, knowing that GOD is unconditional love, and simply wants to give you more of what you are, and that is GOD's Light. By allowing yourself to do this, and to understand without guilt that you can express anger at GOD, and release that anger, and therefore become more in harmony with GOD's Light, for in replacement of that anger you receive GOD's light. You may find that your path becomes smoother.

Question: Spirit, you spoke earlier of our initiation this week. That each of us has gone through an item of initiation. Can you give us some specific examples of what we have experienced to help us understand? Because it seems like an awfully mundane week. It seems like it wasn't any different than anything else.

MASTERS: As we said before, it may seem like a mundane week. For much of what occurs with you happens beneath the surface in terms of your expanding consciousness. For as you know, we work with you when your human consciousness is suspended. For that is when we can work with you most freely, in other words, in your sleep.

There have been subtle shifts in the way you perceive energy in your specific case. There have been subtle shifts to a new operating paradigm in the recesses of your brain, and the way you receive and interpret information. And there have been subtle shifts in the way you react to external stimuli. These shifts have been based on the changes in the way you perceive information. Initiations are not always, should we say, altered-state experiences. Many times initiations come in subtle ways that are subtle to your human mind, but no less profound in terms of the way these initiations move you to a new level of perception, and in the way that these initiations expand your energy to a new level that enables you to accept more light. You have become a bit less prone to internalizing anger, and in reacting to anger. For a part of your consciousness has been healed. The place where you have believed that GOD would withhold from you as has been touched by the Light of Truth. It now knows, in a deep way, that it is always being provided for. With this shift has come a release of the need to express anger and frustration, or to internalize anger and frustration. For you no longer react in anger and frustration when you perceive that you are not being provided for. Every step is a step towards the Light.

Question: I have two questions. I think they are kind of different questions. One is that my week wasn't as mundane. My week was a good week. There were a couple of moments where I just felt absolute joy and knowingness that certain things were going to happen. And I absolutely love that feeling. And my question is how do I maintain that? I'd like to be feeling like that all the time. That's a pretty reasonable thing, don't you think? That's my first question.

I have kind of another question that I was thinking about when you were talking about earlier about the 8-track tape. That happens a lot where I'll be in the middle of something and another idea comes into my head. Sometimes though, they're not pleasant experiences, like the song, "Rejoice." I might be reliving something negative. So I was thinking, "Oh great! An opportunity to change that!" So I really liked what you had to say about that. But I wanted to know if you could talk about that. If going back, or reliving some things that come up, and trying to rewrite them, or replay them in my mind, is going to effect the current thinking? Well it would! Well, I don't know what I'm saying. You probably know it better than me.

MASTERS: We would respond to your second question first, and your first question second. Yes, sometimes that which comes up is that which you were not as well equipped to deal with then as you are now in your position of strength and knowingness. And so now, when you have more tools to work with it, it comes back to the forefront of your consciousness so that you may now release it to the Light. And as you release it to the Light, it effects your here and now. For you no longer have to react to something that happened 20 years ago. In other words, when that seeming traumatic event occurred, what locked into place was a pattern of reaction. And that pattern of reaction repeated itself over years, and years, and years.

But now, there is strength, there is insight, there is help and support so that pattern or reaction can be broken. And so when you work with the root, the event that was at the root of the pattern of reaction, you then no longer have to have the reaction. And therefore, yes, it is good and useful to work with what is brought up. And it will affect your current life. For it breaks down, or eliminates, an old patterning which is no longer serving you.

In the example that we gave for your sister, there was a patterned reaction of anger and frustration because of a core belief that she was not, and would not, be provided for. That belief has shifted. And therefore the reaction is no longer necessary, or prevalent because of the shift in the root cause. Because the core belief has been shifting, and that is a bit of an initiation.

The former portion of your question, you are beginning to experience more and more of the Kingdom of Heaven. You must become acclimated to this place. For it is a place that your human consciousness is not fully comfortable in yet. So you begin by having brief experiences with it. You will continually expand your ability to maintain and sustain your living in the Kingdom of Heaven until that becomes more your natural state of affairs. And your living in anything less than harmony, and confidence, and perfection, and joy and bliss becomes the anomaly. For the more you experience Heaven, the more accustomed you are to it.

What occurs when you initially experience Heaven, is that it is a jolt to your human consciousness. Your human consciousness believes, and fears, that something is wrong, for Heaven is a new state of being. Your human consciousness, or your ego resists because it fears that it will be destroyed if all is moved into the Kingdom of Heaven. It then draws you away from your bliss by creating situations that would either draw your attention, or cause you to doubt that Heaven is sustainable.

However, each time this occurs, you expand your Light more, and more, and more. And we keep talking about a cycle of expansion that is not unlike the downward spiral that the unenlightened portion of your consciousness knows so well. Well, an upward spiral does the same thing. And so in a very natural, and organic, and involuntary way, more and more of your consciousness is propelled into the Kingdom of Heaven. And less and less of your consciousness is mired in what we would dramatically call "Hell on Earth." For the consciousness that you are nurturing, and expanding, and adopting is the consciousness of Heaven. And the consciousness that you were finding no more use for it is the consciousness of pain and suffering. And what is pain and suffering but Hell?

Question: I can feel Spirit. I can feel your energy working with me during the week. And it feels terrific. And I'd like to know if there are any pointers, or ways I'd be able to communicate with you during the week.

MASTERS: You are already doing quite wonderfully with this. For we are able to touch you in your state of suspended consciousness, where we continue these classes with you, and work with you in a very intense way. For these physical classes are simply, and only, a conscious reflection and reminder of what is truly occurring on a different plane of consciousness.

You are continually opening your channel to us, and we are continually feeding you with Light, and energy and healing. And as this process occurs quite naturally, and as you work with the discipline of meditation, you will eventually find that communicating with us is not unlike communicating with a friend or colleague on the earth plane. And you will have and develop relationships with us that are not unlike your relationships on the earth plane.

In summary, what you can do is meditate. Call on our energy in a conscious way. You might also do some writing, which we would call stream of consciousness writing, which is a very subtle way to enable our consciousness and your consciousness to merge. So that our consciousness might eventually, and lovingly, overshadow your consciousness and communicate to you through your own channel.

Question: I feel...I know that either you or my colleagues here get tired of this kind of question. But I would just like to know if I've been on the right track in this last week. Because it feels as if things have come to a standstill as far as diagnosis, much less treatment. And this is of considerable concern to me in various dimensions in my life. And I need help.

MASTERS: You are always on the right track. Remember that every experience that you have is an opportunity to open to the light of GOD that is always available, and this "track" of opening to GOD is in truth the only track and the only purpose for your embodiment. Therefore, have faith that you are constantly moving back home to the heart of GOD. You have the love and support of many beings who are guiding and protecting you through this process. Be blessed and in GOD, for GOD is with you always.

Final Comments

So ends this portion of the journey for the people just like you who participated in these sessions. These people are continuing to take steps toward their enlightenment. They continue to show progress that begins with their internal changes. This internal transformation is then reflected in their outer worlds as more peace, bliss, synchronicity, joy and abundance in every way. This path is open to you too.

This path is fully dependent on you, and how you proceed based on this information. You may choose to use this information simply as an intellectual exercise and place it in the category of "hmmm... that is interesting". You may place it in the category of "I have heard many of these truths before expressed in different ways." Or you may take this information to heart.

By "taking this information to heart" we mean examining your consciousness to see where your consciousness is aligned with GOD's unconditional love and where it is not. By "taking this information to heart" we mean working with the information, in prayer, meditation and emotional release so that the new truths become deeply embedded in your consciousness. As this process occurs, your consciousness is transformed.

You can gather together in groups to discuss the information and support each other in living in accordance with the information provided. You can gather additional information to support this work such as "Pathways to Inner Peace: Lifesaving Processes for Healing Heart, Mind and Soul. Finally, you can, of course, call on the Masters for their direct support.

No matter what the next steps of your process may be, know that you are loved, blessed and protected by the light of GOD. Know that you are innocent and therefore, need not suffer from guilt. Know that you are perfect, and therefore need not judge yourself or live in fear of the judgments of others. Know always that GOD loves you -- just as you are.

Be blessed and in GOD.

Index of Key Concepts